IN THE PIT

A testimony of
God's faithfulness
to a bipolar Christian

Nancy L. Hagerman

Essence
PUBLISHING

Belleville, Ontario, Canada

In the Pit

A Testimony of God's Faithfulness
to a Bipolar Christian

Copyright © 2001, Nancy L. Hagerman

All Scripture quotations, unless otherwise noted, are taken from *The Holy Bible, New International Version* (North American Edition), copyright © 1973, 1978, 1984 by the International Bible Society. Used by permission of Zondervan Publishing House.

Scriptures marked NASV are taken from the *New American Standard Bible*. Copyright © The Lockman Foundation 1960, 1962, 1963, 1968, 1971, 1972, 1973. All rights reserved.

Any special emphasis on certain words or phrases is the author's.

ISBN: 1-55306-200-0
First Printing: March 2001
Second Printing: February 2003

Essence Publishing is a Christian Book Publisher dedicated to further-ing the work of Christ through the written word. For more information, contact: 44 Moira Street West, Belleville, Ontario, Canada K8P 1S3. Phone: 1-800-238-6376. Fax: (613) 962-3055.
E-mail: info@essencegroup.com
Internet: www.essencegroup.com

Printed in Canada
by

Essence
PUBLISHING

To my Lord who is teaching me to stand;
and to my dearest friend and husband, Steve,
who didn't leave, but remembered his promise
at our wedding and stayed by my side
to help pull me out of the pit.

Contents

Acknowledgements

Thank you most of all to Jesus. Without His deliverance there would be no story to tell.

Thanks to my husband for his love and support. He is my hero and a mighty man of God. He lived this book with me and brought to my remembrance many things that had grown fuzzy through the years. He also spent countless hours editing, without which this book would be in sorry shape.

Thanks to my children for allowing me to tell their part of the story. They're great! Thanks to my grandchildren for providing so much illustrative material and just because they love this old grandma as I am.

Thanks to my little sister, "Paula Sue." She is not just a sister but also one of my dearest friends and she has been there to hold my hand from the very beginning. I love you, Sis!

I gratefully acknowledge the many wonderful friends God has granted me. They have been to me as Aaron and

Hur were to Moses. When my hands became too heavy they came alongside and held up my arms, supporting me in the conflict. I won't mention everyone by name or I'd double the size of the book, but I must acknowledge a few:

Jim and Ronnie, Glenn and Mary, Shirley and Glenn, Paul and Kim, Verdis, and the entire precious family at "Spirit of Life" Fellowship. Your prayers and encouragement have accomplished more than you will ever know.

MaryBeth, Carol, and Shirley, who spent hours critiquing and editing manuscripts for me.

Bonny and Glenda, my "cactus" friends.

Katy P. and Mary K., who have always had an ear to lend and a shoulder to cry on. Thanks for your encouragement.

The countless friends who receive our prayer letter and have prayed for our family through the years. God knows what a difference you have made in our lives.

I thank you, too, precious reader. God loves you so much! I pray He blesses you as you read this book. Keep looking up.

Preface

I have tried to write the type of book I wish had been available for me in the first few months of my battle to get well. The struggle may have been somewhat quicker and easier.

For many years I sought freedom from the deep depressions and unexplainable mood swings that haunted me. They colored every relationship—with my husband, my children, my friends, my church, and my God. I believed that if I could only make myself a good enough Christian, I would be able to control my moods.

God was too faithful to allow me to believe that I could do anything in my own strength, apart from Him. He waited until I gave up completely. Until I had absolutely no hope left. Then He climbed down into the pit of despair with me and helped me find my way out.

It has been a long process and a lot of hard work. I haven't achieved perfect wholeness and won't this side of heaven. But He has remained beside me every step of the way.

I continue to experience occasional down times, and sometimes I still feel agitated and excitable. But they only last from a few hours to a day or two, rather than months at a time. Jesus is always right there with me, exhorting me to stand firm and telling me the truth. *I am His child and He will NOT let go of my hand.*

I could praise Him for the rest of eternity and never hope to express everything He means to me! I look forward to the coming day, when, if I have earned any reward, I can lay it at His precious feet and honor Him with all I have. He already gave His all for me.

Bless the Lord, O my soul;
And all that is within me, bless His holy name.
Bless the Lord, O my soul,
And forget none of his benefits;
Who pardons all your iniquities;
Who heals all your diseases;
Who redeems your life from the pit;
Who crowns you with lovingkindness and compassion;
Who satisfies your years with good things,
So that your youth is renewed like the eagle.

Psalm 103:1-5 (NASV)

Part I
The Bottomless Pit

I called on Thy name, O Lord,
Out of the lowest pit.
Thou hast heard my voice....

~ *Lamentations 3:55,56 (NASV)* ~

PROLOGUE

The Healing Begins

Empty, alone, defeated, in pain,
Yet even in the void He is there.
He heals, He loves, He seeks, He protects.
HE IS ALL.
Jesus! Lord of life, Lord of death,
MASTER of my destiny.

~ N.H.

"I can keep silent no longer." The pastor's wife rose to her feet during our prayer time and turned to face the congregation. "God has shown me that there is someone here who feels as if she is in a bottomless pit or a black hole," she stated. "She feels that life is completely hopeless, that she is trapped with no way out, and that God has completely forsaken her."

Her eyes seemed to look straight into mine, as though she knew her message was for me! "God is in that dark pit with you. He is holding you this very moment, and He will deliver you and set your feet upon the solid Rock."

I started to weep uncontrollably as my Savior and my friends began to minister to me. For almost forty years, I had prayed for freedom from the uncontrollable mood swings and dark depressions that haunted my life. Now, I sensed the answer was at hand. The healing had begun....

Just that morning I had discussed the despair I felt with my husband. "I feel like I'm in a bottomless pit or a black hole with no way out. There is no hope left. I don't think I can go on."

It was extremely difficult to even get out of bed, let alone prepare meals or do housework. Life was so heavy, I felt I couldn't bear it any longer.

"The worst of it is that, though I know I've failed you, I've failed God even more. Any decent Christian would shake this off and keep her eyes fixed on Jesus. I don't think He can help me now, because I haven't trusted Him."

I finished with the words my husband had heard many times and come to dread. "I wish I were dead!"

Time and again I had prayed to die and pass into oblivion forever, so I wouldn't have to feel any more. I desired neither heaven nor hell. I simply wanted to float in a sea of nothingness forever. Anything would be better than the constant pain I lived in all the time.

I knew if I killed myself, it would scar my children and they didn't deserve to be hurt. I couldn't live and I couldn't die. I believed myself to be more hopeless than anyone else on earth. "Why would a loving God leave me like this?" I often asked myself.

Most of the first half of my life was spent longing to die. But this book is not about death. It's about finding life in Christ. He has been faithful to me from my mother's womb, so to tell the story I must start from the beginning....

CHAPTER ONE
Childhood

See, Israel's gentle Shepherd stands
With all-engaging charms;
Hark, how He calls the tender lambs,
And folds them in His arms!

~ *Philip Doddridge*

My parents desperately wanted a child. By age thirty-two, my mother had experienced two previous, late-term miscarriages. When she learned she was carrying me she would have done anything to prevent losing a third child. The doctor confined her to bed, and she was not even allowed up to eat or use the lavatory for three months. She said many times that she didn't feel it was a sacrifice because of the joy I brought her.

I entered the world a month early on February 6, 1954, weighing five pounds. "Such a precious tiny bundle," Mom wrote in my baby book. "We had to weigh her every day. When she gained an ounce it was cause for celebration."

My father was in the hospital when I was born, though this was not unusual. He spent a great deal of time there during the course of his life. Upon receiving the telegram announcing my birth, he sent flowers, a bouquet for Mom and another for me. Mama reported that he was "happy and elated".

The doctor required my parents to weigh me without a diaper both before and after feedings. At one point, I'd lost so much weight, the doctor insisted if I lost another ounce I was going back to the hospital. My godly mother prayed most of the night. The next morning I had gained half an ounce and they were allowed to keep me home.

❧

Daddy was an enigma. Though he was never diagnosed as such, I believe he was bipolar and it was passed genetically to me. Sometimes he would be in such a good mood. We played "horsy," bucking up and down while I rode on his back. Alternately he'd swing me high in the air, laughing, tickling and teasing, until we both collapsed in hysterics. As I got older, I noticed there were bad moods, too. I remember him, at times, sitting in the dark, depressed and aloof, and wanting to be left alone.

For a short while, he was youth leader for our church. There were young people coming and going, pizza parties and outings. I always got to go along on their excursions. My Daddy was the king and I felt like a princess.

In the early years, he worked as an encyclopedia salesman. When he returned home in the evening he would often entertain us with funny stories of his daily contacts. No one could be funnier than my Daddy. He was very popular and the life of the party when we went out. Few people, however, knew about his dark side. Mom kept it hidden well, announcing to people that he was "indisposed" and we would not be coming over that evening.

Daddy was disabled with rheumatoid arthritis and collagen disease of an unknown type. He was often in great pain. That was probably the reason the drug abuse began. By the time I was seven or eight years old, he was no longer able to work. He spent most of his time home alone. He would often pick us up after school and take us to a local pharmacy that boasted a soda fountain. While my sister and I enjoyed our sodas with cheese and peanut butter crackers, my father was illegally purchasing prescription pain pills from his "friend," the druggist.

God has since granted me the grace to forgive Dad's friend. I believe he had a certain compassion for my father and was trying to help. He surely had no idea of the real pain he caused our family by these "under the table" dealings with my father.

᯽

By contrast, Mom was a rock. She loved us fiercely and could always be counted on when we needed her, though she worked long hours. She loved to tell the story of how she got her first job.

It had become apparent that my father would not be able to work much longer, so she waited until we went to school and then went job-hunting. She was turned down repeatedly, not because she lacked skills, but had no experience. Her last interview for the day was with a law firm and they asked the question she had heard once too often that day, "Do you have any experience?"

"No!" Mom replied and broke into tears. "And I won't get any either unless someone will hire me." The attorney hired her on the spot and she worked for him until he retired.

It is not easy, even today, for a woman to support a family on her income alone. It was perhaps even more difficult back then, but Mom worked hard and did the best she could. She'd come home from her day job long enough to cook dinner for all of us, then go to her night and weekend job as a medical transcriptionist. An excellent typist, Mom sometimes typed theses for doctoral students from the local university in her "spare" time.

My sister and I loved it when we were allowed to accompany her on the weekend. Her office was perched on a small hill in the middle of a parcel of undeveloped land. We led many jungle safaris and fought off numerous Indian attacks surrounded by the scrub brush outside that office. Mostly, we just enjoyed the opportunity to commandeer a little of Momma's time and attention.

There was never a doubt in my mind that I was deeply loved. I remember Momma often holding me close and whispering that she knew she could never give me everything she wanted, but she prayed constantly that I would always remember that I held her heart. No two girls would ever be more loved than my sister and I. Momma, as you sit at the feet of Jesus now, please know that you gave us everything we needed!

Mom said I eagerly awaited the birth of my little sister, twenty-three months younger than I. Up to that time, I had been raised with a magnificent boxer dog named Old Chris. Mom only had to tell him to watch me, and he would not allow me out of the room. If I tried to crawl under him, he would lay down, and if I tried to climb over him, he'd stand back up. When all else failed, he'd simply grab me by the diaper and haul me back where I belonged. When our landlord insisted that my parents get rid of him, I was heartbroken. At the time, I was simply told they gave him away so they could get me a baby sister to play with.

When she came home from the hospital, I demanded to be allowed to hold "my baby," and she carried that title for some time. I instinctively knew that she was helpless and needed to be cared for. Even at my young age, I assumed it was my responsibility to protect her. She was always "my Paula Sue," even though she became quite annoying when she got old enough to crawl around and take my toys away. At one point, I asked Mom if we couldn't take her back and get Old Chris. But Mom stood her ground. Sis, if you read this, I'm glad she did!

❧

I don't know exactly why I began to feel responsible for my Mom and Dad in addition to my sister. I felt sorry for Dad. I knew he never felt good. Perhaps I saw how hard my Mom worked and wanted to help. More likely, I just loved my parents and desperately wanted to please them.

I started doing all I could to ease Mom's load. The house was vacuumed and dusted, the bathrooms cleaned, the floors swept and mopped, when Mom came home. I was still very young and things weren't always done well, but Mom would praise me—so I kept it up.

The child had begun to parent the parents—a dangerous reversal of roles. Satan would use it to plant a firm belief in the depths of my being that the value of my life was based on my performance.

As long as I did "good deeds," I was worthy of acceptance. If I did not attempt to meet the needs of those around me, I was lazy and self-centered and completely unworthy of love.

I can't describe how good it was to learn that Jesus loves me simply because of who I am, never because of what I do. He has never said to someone earnestly seeking Him, "If you are good, you can be My child." His heart says, "You are My child, let Me help you be good."

I often sing a little verse to my granddaughters and pray it will sink into the depths of their being. It goes like this:

Jesus loves me when I'm good,
When I do the things I should.
Jesus loves me when I'm bad,
Though it makes Him very sad.

~Author unknown

As I grew older, I began to prepare supper for Mom. Sometimes she would drop me off at the grocery store, with her wallet and a list I had made out, so I could do the grocery shopping. When I was finished, I would call her and she would pick me up. Though my mother had never told me so, I was firmly convinced that I had to earn my keep. It would have broken her heart if she had known the truth.

Daddy was not well, and I felt I had to take care of him, too. I remember clearly the time he decided to drive to the store for more cigarettes after he had taken a handful of pills. When he returned, he informed me, "Honey, there's an awful mess for you to clean up in the car." He had vomited all over the windshield, the dash, the steering wheel, and the front seat. I cleaned it up without question. It needed to be done.

Daddy was a heavy smoker. With all the pills he took, he would sometimes become groggy and fall asleep with a cigarette in his hand. I was about eleven when he set the bed on fire while he was still in it. He began screaming and I ran to his room. He had taken so many pills, he couldn't get out of bed by himself. I smothered the fire with pillows, but the smoke was extremely thick and Daddy was too heavy for me to move. I was so ashamed when I had to bother Mom at work to come and make him get out of the smoky room. She didn't mind. In fact, she felt guilty that I had been placed in such a position. But I didn't understand that at the time. I only knew that I was supposed to take care of them, and I had failed them both. Our roles had already been reversed and it was too late to change. I was now the "Caregiver."

As I grew older, I continued to take on more and more responsibility. Momma would say proudly, "I just don't know how I would ever get along without my Nancy," and I would try that much harder to please her. My parents never set out to dump this burden on me. They had no idea how Satan was twisting truth around in my head.

God had His hand on my life, in spite of Satan's deception. I was blessed with godly grandparents, aunts, and uncles who prayed for me even before I was born. God heard them and He was working. Soon I came to realize that something was wrong. No matter how compliant and helpful I was on the outside, I knew my attitudes were far from right on the inside.

In Sunday School I had learned well the message of Matthew 5:48, "*be perfect, therefore, as your heavenly*

Father is perfect." Being a natural perfectionist, I had taken it to heart. I tried to be picture perfect in my thoughts and actions, but I always ended up like the man Paul described in Romans 7:19: "*For what I do is not the good I want to do; no, the evil I do not want to do—this I keep on doing.*" I knew selfishness and anger were wrong. Although they didn't show in my actions, they were very real in my heart. I could not control them.

I was about fourteen when I had an unusual dream. A large purple throne filled with light descended from heaven into our front yard. The final judgment was here. I was terrified and couldn't rejoice, as I knew a Christian should. Christians were supposed to look forward to Christ's return and reigning forever with Jesus. But all I could do was cower behind a small bush. Even then, I knew He could see me and I was neither worthy nor ready.

I knew in my heart that, if I were judged at that moment, I would be found wanting. For the first time, I began to consider hell and started asking people how someone could be absolutely sure they were going to heaven.

One incident still stands out in my memory. When I was fifteen, I spent the night with my girlfriend. We ate until we were both ready to burst, giggled a lot, and when the house got quiet, we got serious. I confessed to her my confusion and asked if she had any answers. Her reply was remarkable, "Nancy, I don't know any more about it than you do, but it seems to me that if we were going to heaven, we would be sure!" From that day, my quest began in earnest.

Every night I'd plead with God to show me how to go to heaven. It wasn't long before that "still, small voice" spoke to me as I knelt in the dark. "My precious child, I have already taken care of everything necessary for you to spend eternity in heaven. All you need to do is trust in Me." I cannot put into words the joy that flooded my being. Was it really so simple? I could not have explained the doctrine of salvation, or how Jesus' death had freed me from the law of sin and death, but in my childish mind I decided to take Him at His Word. He set me free at that moment. I belonged to Him!

℘

Only a little while later, I had an exceptionally trying day with my father and went to bed early. I knelt at the side of my bed, in tears, unable to pray except to plead, "Please help me!" I cried myself to sleep. Although I couldn't feel God, He was there.

That night, I had a dream. I was in a room full of people having a celebration. I was kneeling alone in a corner and weeping. Jesus came into the room and everyone rushed to greet Him. Everyone but me. I was ashamed because I was crying and just could not make myself joyful right then. Jesus spent no time with any of the others, though He was never rude to anyone. Smiling and touching people lightly, He walked past them and headed straight toward me. He wore a long robe, full of light that was so bright I couldn't see His face. As I knelt in the corner, trying to hide, He laid both hands on my head, looked up, and said, "Father, this little lamb of ours needs us so much right now." With that, I awakened with a tremendous sense of peace. It was one of my first conscious revelations of God's faithfulness to me.

I don't share this experience to boast or make anyone feel they lack faith if they have never had a dream about

Jesus. Perhaps it's the weaker among us who need more concrete experiences. I don't begin to understand all of God's ways. I only know that, though God deals with each of us differently, treating us as the individuals we are, He loves every one of us equally, and gave His life to prove it. We are all His precious ones.

CHAPTER TWO
Marriage

My beloved is mine, and I am his.

~ Song of Songs 2:16 (NASV)

As far back as I can remember, I wanted to be a doctor. After my conversion, I decided I would become a medical missionary. Our church gave tuition scholarships to members who wanted to attend Bible College; so when I graduated from high school, I packed my things and drove with my family to Intermountain Bible College in Grand Junction, Colorado.

I felt intense guilt about leaving my sister to hold down the fort at home. Caring for Mom and Dad was my responsibility. I knew that Mom, especially, but Dad, too, would miss me terribly; however, my loyalties were with Jesus by then. I had to obey what I thought He was asking of me.

As my folks prepared to drive back to New Mexico, my mother said she had forgotten something and ran back inside. It wasn't until they were gone that I returned to my dormitory room and discovered that she had placed "Pinkie" on my bed. He was a very ragged, pink stuffed lamb that I'd slept with throughout my childhood. That night, I held him tight and cried myself to sleep. My sister tells me that, back home, she heard a strange noise in the night and checked my room. She found my mother holding another of my stuffed animals and weeping. Growing up can be tough for everyone involved.

I loved Bible College. This one was very small, with less than 100 students. Because I worked in the kitchen for my board, I knew almost everyone. It was so good to be surrounded by people who wanted to serve the Lord as much as I did. Of course, some were there for fun and games, or to get away from home, but there was a good solid core of young people there to learn about Jesus. Sometimes we would have impromptu prayer meetings when the desire to pray would strike several of us at the same time. We'd find each other waiting in the chapel. These usually went on late, but we were always mightily blessed and experienced many answers to those prayers. God was teaching us about His faithfulness to His children.

Bipolar disorder began to rear its head while I was in college, though I didn't recognize it at the time. Sometimes I was popular and happy, everyone's friend and confidant. But just as suddenly, my mood would go dark. At those times, I had trouble believing even God could really love someone as worthless as I knew I was. I became convinced my friends were only being nice to me because they were Christians and felt they had to be kind. I doubted my salvation and became certain that I had blown it. There remained, for me, "no further sacrifice for sin." I could expect only judgment for my "wickedness." My mood would soon change then again, and I'd return to being friendly and well-liked.

℘ↄ

I had many friends among the boys, but no boyfriend. In fact, I had never dated, except to go to my senior prom with a younger boy who lived down the street from us. (Our mothers didn't want me to miss it.) Most of the boys at college treated me like a big sister, wanting me to ask one of the other girls if they would go out with them. I usually didn't mind. I had decided I would give up marriage for Jesus, in order to serve Him better. Still, sometimes I felt so alone. At those times, I would usually pray, seeking God's will. I knew I wanted to be a missionary, but didn't know where. God always corrected me gently, whispering that He wanted me to be a missionary wife. Didn't He understand that I wanted to honor Him by remaining single? How foolish we can be when we are determined to make God fit into our little box! He has so many wonderful gifts to bestow, if we will only let Him be God and trust that He knows best.

My freshman year passed quickly. Toward the end of that year, we had some special speakers in chapel. They came to tell us about Turkey, a country I knew little about. There was a young woman and two young men, but the one that caught my eye was dark-haired, blue-eyed, and very handsome. (He still is!)

He told us that Turkey was "a Bible land without the Bible." He pointed out that Paul was born in Turkey (Tarsus), and that the sites of the seven churches of Revelation are there. Antioch, where the disciples were first

27

called Christians, and Mt. Ararat, where Noah's ark landed, are located in Turkey. I was surprised to learn that most of the New Testament was written to cities there. I even had a map of Turkey, in the back of my Bible, with Paul's missionary journeys traced on it.

It was heartbreaking to learn that this Bible land was now over 99 percent Muslim and less than ten Turkish Christians were known to exist at that time. He detailed a ministry he had founded, in which Christians could mail gospel letters into the country. Addresses were obtained from the phone book. This would sift out people who were really interested, so workers in Turkey could concentrate their efforts on them and lessen the risk that they would be discovered and thrown out of the country. I had found a calling.*

Though I never considered that he might be available to me, I was quite taken with the dark-haired young man. I assumed that he was already spoken for, or dedicated to singleness, as I was. He had beautiful blue eyes, and I appreciated his commitment to and deep love for God. I told the Lord that, if I ever did marry, I wanted someone just like him.

 howdy

I took some literature home and promptly filed it away in my desk to be dealt with "later." It wasn't until the next year, when I returned as a sophomore, that the Lord began to remind me of the literature I had picked up and the sorrow I'd felt for Turkey. When He woke me one night from a sound sleep and made the burden too intense to ignore any longer, I realized He was serious. He meant NOW! The

---

* For more information about this ministry see Appendix III.

following morning, I dug out the pamphlet I had picked up so many months ago, and called the number on it.

By this time, the young man who had spoken, the founder of Friends of Turkey (FOT), had moved. He was pastoring a church in a small town about sixty miles away. Little did I know he had recently confessed to the women's prayer group that he was lonely and wanted a wife. They had been praying that very night.

He had left some friends in charge of the FOT office in Grand Junction when he moved, but for some reason, they didn't find time to get any literature to me. When I continued to call, they were impressed that I was so serious and suggested that Steve should come down and speak with me himself. The very next weekend, with the ladies group still praying, he drove in to town.

I was delighted to see the box of gospel letters he brought for me. Of course, it was also thrilling to see him again. He fascinated me. We visited a while before he handed over the box of letters and asked if I could get the folks in my church to mail them. His spirituality and single-minded love for the Lord impressed me all over again.

He told me later that he had been highly impressed with me, also. He'd wondered if God might be putting us together, but he had met another girl earlier in the week and was uncertain of God's direction. His church had continued to pray for a wife for him. He wanted to be very sure he was walking with God and not running ahead of Him. On the other hand, I still assumed he was unavailable but sure hoped there was another one like him somewhere around.

I learned all I could about Turkey and Islam, spoke at church, and distributed gospel letters. I didn't see Steve again for months.

Our college had an annual Christmas banquet. The restaurant we had chosen that year had inadvertently booked two parties at the same time, so we put our banquet off until January. Everyone was lining up their dates and I was busy playing big sister to all the guys by finding out if the girl they liked would go out with them. I was the only person left without a date. Friends encouraged me to go anyway, but I was ashamed and too insecure to be the only single person there. I chose to stay home and throw myself a pity-party.

I knelt before the Lord and cried out, "WHY?" He knew I had given Him my heart and never planned to marry. But did that mean never having a date, never enjoying a hug or kiss from someone who thought me special, walking alone through the rest of my life? I wrestled with the Lord for some time until I finally gave in. "Okay, Lord, it's really You I want more than anything. If Your will is for me to be exclusively Yours, then although I've already forsaken marriage, I now forsake dating, too. I choose to be completely Yours." I climbed into bed with tears drying on my cheeks. I was content.

A knock on the door awakened me early the next morning. Much to my surprise, when I opened it, I discovered the handsome young missionary who had given me the gospel letters to distribute. My heart skipped a beat as I realized how I must look. I had on an old, tattered housecoat and my hair flew in fifty different directions. I had a cold, so my nose was red and stuffy and my eyes watered. Then I remembered I had given up dating. It didn't matter anyway, so I invited him in.

I was sure he had come to see how I was doing with the gospel letters and to ask if I needed more. But I was in for a surprise. He knocked my socks off when he asked me to go out with him! I shot a speedy prayer skyward and received quick assurance that this was okay.

Often in my life, God has required me to give up something that I hold very dear. He often gives it back once it is surrendered, but this was almost beyond belief. Not only had I put all men aside for Jesus just last night, but the next morning I learned that this man, whom I was extremely attracted to, had noticed me and wanted me to go out with him!

On that first date, Steve took me to dinner. A new dress, mailed by my mother, had arrived that day. There was no special reason. She simply wanted to surprise me. I considered it an extra blessing from the Father. Steve and I talked many hours that evening, but he was careful to get me home before curfew. I was enchanted. He loved my Lord so fervently. At the ripe old age of eighteen, I was in love.

§⥾

We had our first date on January 31, 1973. By Easter of that same year, we were engaged. I had trouble believing I was worthy to marry him and tried to break up a few times, but he finally convinced me it was okay that I wasn't perfect. (I learned soon enough that he wasn't, either.) We were married in September of that year.

We opted to be married outdoors at one of our favorite places, the Colorado National Monument. The Monument is a huge mountain of rock, with canyons running from end to end. A highway winds its way up and over the top, often right along the rim of a deep gorge. Steve and I liked to spend time there and found a beautiful spot for the wedding. Ute Canyon Overlook was accessed by a short trail lined with piñon trees and wildflowers. The Overlook, itself, was a piece of rock that ended in a sheer cliff at the edge of the canyon. The view was absolutely gorgeous. It made a perfect spot for a wedding ceremony.

A record-breaking storm blew through western Colorado on the eve of our wedding. While planning the event, I'd called the library to find out what time sunset would occur on that day. I meant when the sky would turn a magnificent crimson. I was given the time when our corner of the world would be plunged into darkness. It proved to be an interesting wedding, as I tripped down the aisle, lighted only by the few lanterns Steve's brother had been able to borrow. My veil swirled around my head like a helicopter rotor and the wind whipped the little hair my Dad had left until it stuck straight out on both sides. Photos of our wedding show people grimacing from the cold with the tendons sticking out on their necks. My mother stopped Steve, as he approached the front, to whisper that the communion bread had blown over the cliff and down the canyon. Steve says we partook of "hidden manna" that evening, as we pretended to take our first communion together as man and wife.

We had written our own vows, but as the clouds gathered over our heads and the wind grew worse, the preacher began leaving out more and more of the ceremony. He barely had time to say, "You may kiss the bride," when the storm broke and everyone ran for cover. The wind uprooted trees that evening, but we laughed when we remembered the last line of the poem we had printed in our program: "But when the storm is gone, we know He leads us on."

We had to chuckle again the next morning, when we opened our devotional book. The text was taken from Matthew 7:24-27:

> *Therefore everyone who hears these words of Mine, and puts them into practice, is like a wise man who built his house on the rock. The rain came down, the streams rose, and the winds blew and beat against that house, yet it did not fall, because it had its foundation on the Rock....*

CHAPTER THREE
Motherhood

Halfway up the stairs
Isn't up,
And isn't down.
It isn't in the nursery,
It isn't in the town.
And all sorts of funny thoughts
Run round my head:
"It isn't really
Anywhere!
It's somewhere else
Instead!"
~ A.A. Milne,
When We Were Very Young

We became parents on November 18, 1975. My mother called a few days earlier, wondering how I was feeling. She said she had a dream that I'd phoned and told her I had a little, blue-eyed boy, named Jason. The previous night, Steve and I had decided on the name, Jason. Since none of our parents had approved of a single name that we'd brought up, we had decided this one would be a surprise. So much for that!

Mom was right. In a few days, I held my blue-eyed boy named Jason. I had not known that my heart could ever hold so much love. I wanted to spend the rest of my life taking care of him.

The doctor said that newborn babies were sleepy and that, when we got home, we should put him to bed and let him rest. We laid him in his crib and he began to cry. Steve decided that he must be wet and, being a modern father, decided to change him. I was to rest. Only a few minutes passed before I heard Steve screaming for help. Jason had "sprinkled" his father, the crib, the walls, and everything else within about eight feet. I think he wanted us to know up front just who was in charge now.

Jason was a difficult baby. He had colic and multiple allergies from day one. He demanded to be fed every two hours around the clock. After feeding, he would sleep for half an hour and then wake up to be entertained until it was time to eat again. Sometimes, I felt he deliberately slept no more than six hours in twenty-four simply so he could keep me awake. I began to think I would lose my mind, and cried much of the time for days on end.

Mental illness often strikes in young adulthood. Though I had experienced some symptoms in college, it now hit much harder. My husband didn't know whom he was coming home to from day to day. Would it be Mary Poppins or the Wicked Witch of the West? He did his best, but neither of us knew what we were dealing with. We attributed it to "baby blues."

I went to my parent's house for a week of rest and Mom became frightened and worried, too. I was no longer the kind, thoughtful girl she remembered. I was irritable, surly, and very moody.

I had trained myself, early in life, to believe that the personal happiness of everyone I loved was my responsibility. And I loved my baby.

Psychologists call this *codependency*, but I had not heard the term back then. I only knew that being a good mother meant committing myself, twenty-four hours a day, to cater to Jason's every whim. I was exhausted, with nothing left to give. No one can be everything to another person, but codependent people often believe that, if they only try hard enough, they should be able to. If only I had known that once his basic needs were met, it was all right to take care of me. When I could not meet the artificial goal I'd set for myself, I began to question why God had made me a mother.

Satan convinced me I was a rotten wife, a terrible mother, and a Christian who didn't deserve to bear the name. How could God love me any longer when, in my mind, I had been a terrible wife to the wonderful man He had given me, and when sometimes the mother in me wanted to walk away and leave that baby crying in his crib?

❦

In bipolar illness, you create your own reality. That alone is real, rather than what anyone else might tell you. The truth is only what you perceive it to be. Without a doubt, I knew I was a "total failure." Suicide began to look like my only option for escape, although concerns about what might come after death gave me serious reason for pause.

I really didn't care about going to heaven. Living forever didn't appeal to me because life, as I saw it, was full of pain and hopelessness. The idea of passing into nothingness enticed me, but I knew eternity would be spent in either heaven or hell. Someone told me once that suicide victims went to hell. Though I couldn't be sure about that, I knew I didn't want to end up there; so I couldn't risk making God any angrier with me than I thought He already was. He used my doubts to keep me alive.

I thought it would be best for me to leave, in order to set Steve free from the terrible person I believed myself to be. I knew, however, that it would wound him and his ministry to Turkey, and my heart would never allow me to put Jason elsewhere for a while. I was so confused. In my mind, the kindest thing to do would be to rid my family of myself. I also knew by doing that, I would hurt them.

Even Steve didn't understand how ill I really was. I told him, over and over, what a terrible mother I was and that I was afraid it would ruin Jason to be raised by someone like me. Steve tried to reassure me, but I could not hear him. The reality I had created for myself told me that I was bad. I was a bad mother, a bad wife, a bad Christian, and a bad person. As such, I was unworthy and deserved nothing. Anyone who tried to tell me differently was only being kind because they thought they had to be. I knew the truth about myself.

If only I had realized at the time that it was not a sign of weakness or lack of spirituality for Christians to seek help for mental illness! Many of us accept it as perfectly normal to see a doctor when our bodies are sick, but believe it's unspiritual to get help when our minds are sick. And so we suffer unspeakable pain, while we continue to smile and say, "I'm fine!" when anyone asks.

There was, unquestionably, a faulty belief system at work in my life. The truth is that God was never disappointed in me. He never thought I was a lousy wife and a worse mother. He may have been sad because I listened to and believed Satan's lies, instead of looking to the Creator, the One who held all the answers. But He never condemned me. He simply continued drawing me toward Himself. I didn't understand how much God cherished me exactly the way I was. I forgot my worth was not based on my performance, but on Jesus' shed blood. I was too immature to realize that truth is rarely in the way we feel. Truth is in the Word of God.

The Word calls Satan "the accuser of the brethren." It also tells us that he is deceitful above all things. Jesus Himself called him a liar and murderer. Satan will stop at nothing to hurt and destroy. His goal is to see us all in hell. The only way the devil can gain victory is if we refuse to claim our rightful place as children of God and take our stand against him. We overcome by the blood of the Lamb and by the word of our testimony (Revelation 12:11). We use both our position in Christ and the Word of Truth to defeat our enemy. As we resist the devil, he will flee from us.

ЯЭ

At that point in time, the high place I held at the right hand of Jesus was something I was not aware of. My eyes were so much on myself—and my performance—that I never took a stand. Satan shook me like a rag doll.

The Prince of Darkness doesn't often put glaring temptation in a Christian's way. Obvious tactics rarely work. He lies. He accuses us in our minds.

He whispers, *You're a terrible Christian. How could God ever forgive you again?*

He says things like, *You are so fat, (skinny, homely, and so forth)... You are absolutely no good to God or anyone else. You are completely unacceptable.*

A favorite lie is: *You'll have to try harder if you really want God to love you. Christ died for you and just look how often you fail Him. YOU'RE WORTHLESS!*

There are many lies he uses, and all of us have heard some. The problem is that, because they appear to come from our own thoughts, we believe them. We don't recognize them as lies whispered by Absolute Evil.

The monarch of hell is always a liar and full of deceit. But we need not be afraid, because the Creator of the Universe has already defeated him. We need only to continually remind ourselves of that, and keep our eyes fixed on Jesus.

When Jesus is drawing us to a higher level, He is forever a gentleman. He is the bridegroom. He woos, He encourages, and He draws us to Himself with His extraordinary love. He never criticizes or condemns us. Romans 8:1 says, *"Therefore there is now no condemnation for those who are in Christ Jesus."* The Author and Perfecter of our Faith (Hebrews 12:2) *gently* convicts and teaches us that we can be more. He empowers us with freedom to grow and become what we were created to be. It fills my heart to overflowing to be loved by a Lord such as this!

Author's Note: As I worked on this section, the computer deleted the above paragraph and shut itself down three times. Finally, I thought to ask God to intervene. That was the end of it. I believe there is something here the devil does not want Christians to think about.

℅

As my son grew, we discovered he was hyperactive and very strong-willed. He comes from a family of determined and strong-minded people, including patriots who planned and fought the Revolutionary War, some who worked on the Underground Railroad, and even pro-life picketers of today. Many of these fine people, then and now, have taken their stand in Jesus' name against the status quo. They believed it was what God wanted. We were proud of Jason's heritage. My mother commented that, "he hadn't sucked that strong will out of his thumb!"

Jason's first word was, naturally, "No!" Steve was pastoring a church at the time and we had attended a revival meeting hosted by another fellowship in the area. The visiting evangelist was a hellfire-and-brimstone preacher. The sermon thundered to a climax with the question, "Is there anyone in this room who can honestly say they have been saved?" At that very moment, my small son, who was trying hard to tear a page out of one of the hymnals and getting very impatient at my interference with his plans, screamed out, "NO!" We slipped out with red faces and allowed the revival to continue without Jason's input.

I loved that boy with absolute passion and I love him just as much today. Even in the best frame of mind, a strong-willed child is difficult to raise, and I was not at all healthy emotionally.

Most children will back off when the line is clearly drawn in the dirt. My small son would continually step over it and dare me to do something about it. I always did, but it never kept him from pushing again the next time our wills clashed. I love, pray for, and respect James Dobson of *Focus on the Family*. But I think even he would have found that little boy a challenge.

My three-year-old granddaughter is very much like Jason. Today, I enjoy her spunk when she chooses to exert her independence against an adult twice her size and just say "No!" Her mother has recently married and, because children reflect what they hear, her "No" has been tempered down to "No, honey," but she means it every bit as much! As her Grandma, I find her adorable. When I was the Mommy, it wasn't the least bit cute or funny. I doubted whether I had any parenting skills at all.

During this time, I began feeling weak and tired. I went to our doctor only to learn that I was pregnant again. Jason was nine months old.

ॐ

I'm ashamed to confess that I went home and moved our furniture around, hoping to lose the baby. When that didn't work, I again considered ending my life, but I was afraid. I often felt afraid to live and afraid to die. Everything was so utterly hopeless! I prayed for God to take away my eternity and just send me into nothingness, but I knew He wouldn't answer a prayer like that. Eternity is a gift He has given to be enjoyed by His children, not one to be thrown away. God's gifts are always meant for our good. We simply need to trust Him.

Today I praise God for sending Ruth to me, and for protecting her from my stupidity. At the time, she and my son became two of my few reasons for living. She is a delightful, funny, compassionate woman. In addition, she has blessed us with two precious granddaughters who have become the light of our lives. Children are truly a gift from the Lord!

Ruth was born on June 1, 1977. She was a mellow, quiet baby. We hardly realized she was there. For the first two weeks I was on the phone with the doctor almost daily, wondering what was wrong with her because she slept so much, and rarely cried! He would laugh and tell me to enjoy her. Nowadays, I love nothing better than sitting down and snuggling a grandbaby. As a young mother, I took myself and my "to do" list so seriously that cuddling babies felt like a waste of precious time. I didn't allow myself the enjoyment God meant me to have. Nevertheless, life went on. Steve and I continued to muddle through, now with two babies.

When Ruth was six weeks old, Steve felt God was telling him to resign his pastorate and promote the Turkish ministry full time. We had no regular funds coming in to support the work, so we drove to Colorado and moved in with his parents. It was only two weeks before Steve somehow convinced the bank to loan us money for a house. He worked at many part-time jobs, even doing janitorial work for the Bible College where he had applied to teach.

Finally, he was offered some office space in another ministry's building. We had understood that he would help them in development part-time while receiving a salary and having time to work with Friends of Turkey, too. The salary fell through, but he still spent the day in the office developing the Turkish work.

There was a grocery store a block away, and Steve would check the dumpster most nights for food. He would often bring home milk, bread, and dented cans to share with the neighborhood, but times were still hard and I worried about our babies. God was teaching us to be humble and trust Him: a lesson I didn't want to learn.

One day I began to plead with God. "Please make Steve forget about developing the Turkish ministry and go get a regular job. I am so tired of never knowing where our next meal may come from. I love him, but I need some security."

As I prayed, I saw a picture in my mind of two ropes. One of them was tied to a sturdy oak tree. The other ascended into the sky with no visible means of support. God spoke to me and asked, "Nancy, which of these two ropes do you want to climb on? The one tied to the strong tree, or the one I'm holding?" OUCH! The choice wasn't really a hard one. Everyone knows tree limbs can break, while God is forever faithful.

I knew God was asking for my trust and an acknowledgment that I recognized He would never let me down. I chose the rope He was holding, and begged forgiveness for being selfish. I've never been sorry.

My new-found trust was soon tested. Only a short time later, I ran out of milk for Ruth. There was no money to buy more. She was crying, Jason was hungry, and the refrigerator was empty. I called Steve at his office and held Ruth up to the phone. He started home, but on his way, spotted a parked trailer that held a traveling Christian bookstore. Impressed to stop, he went in.

As he looked around, a man approached him, placed a $20 bill in his hand, and said, "God told me to give you this." Steve thanked him, drove to the grocery store and came home. In those days, twenty dollars would buy a week's worth of groceries. I made him tell the story over and over again. There was much praise and rejoicing that night, as we marveled at how God had provided for us.

ℬ

The children continued to grow—Jason, so much like me, and Ruth, so much like her Daddy. Strong-willed Jason was bright, independent, and active. We nicknamed him "General Patton." Ruth was strong-willed, too, and equally bright, but quieter and more manipulative. She loved to be a part of whatever her brother was doing. We called her, "Princess MeToo." It was fun to watch their early experiences with God and His faithfulness to them.

Ruth had developed an absolute passion for cats, but her brother was allergic to them. We'd tried to let her have outdoor cats, but they didn't stay around. She longed for a pet and announced, one night, that she was going to pray for a kitty. I was concerned and tried to explain again why we couldn't have a kitty, but she was adamant. She bowed her head and prayed, "God please send me a white kitty." The next morning, while Steve and I, ("O ye of little faith") were trying to figure out how to ease her disappointment, we heard her shout. On our back porch were a white mother cat and two white kittens! We had never seen them before, but found out later they lived in the house behind us. The kittens eventually strayed away, but the mother cat stayed around and came to our house every day just before Ruth got home from school. The neighbor finally gave her to Ruth and she lived to be a very old cat. She moved with us several times, always remaining close to Ruth.

The combination of two strong temperaments made for extreme sibling rivalry. I found myself living in what felt like a war zone much of the time. When they weren't in competition with one another, they were usually best friends. Ruth often supplied the mischievous ideas. Jason, though he had plenty of ideas of his own, supplied the muscle to carry them out. They were the bane of baby-sitters, one time locking a girl out of the house, and another time giving a reverse mohawk to our Malamute puppy while the sitter was in another room.

While they were still preschoolers, Steve went on a six-week trip to Turkey. I missed him desperately, and on the day of his return, I scrubbed the house from top to bottom. I showered, washed my hair, and put the kids into a bath. Everything had to be just perfect. I dressed them in their nicest outfits and sent them out to play while I did my make-up before going to the air-port. In less than two minutes, I heard Ruth crying. There was a shallow irrigation ditch in our back yard, which the kids usually ignored. That night, it was over-flowing and filled with glorious mud. Someone had thrown the first handful and now they were both com-pletely covered in slime. To this day, they both insist the other one started it first.

I became hysterical and called my mother. I was so overwrought I could not speak, but only cried into the phone. My mother thought Steve's plane must have crashed and was quickly becoming frantic herself, when I managed to tell her about the mud fight. She began laughing hysterically (the traitor) at the picture of her two bedraggled grandchildren and their frazzled mother.

I took myself so seriously then. Now I laugh as hard as Mom did when I remember those muddy faces. At the time, I angrily hosed the children down in the back yard and changed their clothes. We made it to the airport with time to spare. Every time I called my mother for the next few weeks, she'd begin snickering into the telephone.

I love my children with all my heart, both now and then, and cherish them as gifts from God Himself. The stress and depression I was experiencing had nothing to do with them. It existed because my worth was not based on who I was in Christ, but on how well I performed. I had to be in control of the externals of my environment at all times, or I was a failure.

As the mud episode illustrates, it is totally impossible to keep small children and a home in perfect control at all times. The harder I tried, the more I failed. Stress built inside me like a pressure cooker on high heat. And because I had a very real illness, which was precipitated by stress, I constantly felt as though I was about to break.

I still believed the lie that I had to work harder and make myself better, in order for God to forgive me again and restore me to fellowship with Him. It's impossible to express the depth of my despair during that time. I longed for God, but was wholly convinced I was unworthy. Satan would even use Scripture against me to prove how hopeless my situation was.

Daily he would remind me of Hebrews 6:4-6:

> *It is impossible for those who have once been enlightened, who have tasted the heavenly gift, who have shared in the Holy Spirit, who have tasted the goodness of the word of God and the powers of the coming age, if they fall away, to be brought back to repentance, because to their loss they are crucifying the Son of God all over again and subjecting Him to public disgrace (Emphasis mine).*

I realize, now, that to fall away, as mentioned in the verses above, doesn't mean to stumble or be imperfect. It is a total and complete rejection of God and an absolute resolve to choose one's own way until death, in spite of the knowledge of grace. Even then, the Shepherd seeks His lost lamb and tries to woo her back because of His amazing love. Nonetheless, in those days, I believed that whenever I was cross with my husband, impatient with my children, or thought of myself before others, I was crucifying my Lord again.

Horrible mood swings plagued me. The depressive mood was more prevalent, but the manic times came, too. Sometimes I would get extreme bursts of energy. My mind would begin to spin with worries, plans, and ideas coming one on top of the other. I would be absolutely helpless to slow down. I talked incessantly, and often slept for only a few hours or not at all. Sometimes I would lose my car in a shopping center parking lot, or forget where I was, because I could not concentrate. At times like these, I often felt a need to write things down. In fact, I had been in the habit of writing letters to God since my college years because it seemed that, whether I was in a state of depression or mania, I had trouble holding a thought in my mind long enough to finish a prayer. In 1986, I wrote:

> *Does living the consecrated life have to be this way: one trial or discipline after another with no reprieve? Must it mean constant vigilance against self—with constant lying down on the altar of sacrifice? Is there never any time for joy? Any time for rest? Can one never put the battle away for a brief time—or at least have one's hands supported like Aaron and Hur did for Moses? Will I*

*never feel happy or content again or will it always
be this constant discipline to surrender self and
break the old man? I feel so alone and so tired. I
wonder if I'll ever be broken and useful or if I am
so hard that this will go on and on for the rest of
my life? If so, I hope it ends soon! Where have all
the romance, and the fun, and the joy in life gone?
Everything is misery and struggle.*

A good friend saw me writing the above quote and
read a little over my shoulder. She told me that what I
had written was not true. That I was one of the godliest
people she knew. As a result, I was convinced my friend
didn't really know me at all. It never dawned on me that
perhaps I was confused and she was telling the truth.

As I mentioned before, people in the throes of mental
illness only believe the reality they have created for themselves. Even though I thought I was worthless to God, He
loved me too much to allow me to continue believing the
lies. He understood my illness and knew I had reached
my limit. Though I was too weak, immature, and
ashamed to seek His help, He knew my need. When He
couldn't get my attention through my friends... when I
only read His Word to prove to myself that I was right...
He allowed a crisis to get my attention.

❧

Stress is a main trigger to bipolar illness, and something just about any psychiatrist will tell you to try to
avoid. My codependent compulsion to meet all the
needs of everyone around me, along with my drive to
be totally perfect, brought about an unbelievable
amount of stress.

One afternoon, I blew. On the outside, I was unusually calm. I made sure the kids were occupied elsewhere and got dinner prepared and ready to be heated up. Then, I stepped out into the garage, closed all the windows, got into the car and turned it on.

Scenes from my short life passed before my eyes, and I began to weep. I simply could not betray my husband and children this way. I loved them too much. I turned the car off, went back in the house and called Steve for help. He must have sensed the urgency in my voice, because he left work and came straight home to get me to a doctor.

My Christian doctor told Steve I was depressed and he wanted to put me on some medication. I resisted the idea, believing that if I could just trust the Lord enough, everything would be all right.

The doctor explained that our brain communicates with itself by sending electrical impulses through neurons. These neurons don't actually touch one another. The electric impulses are carried from one neuron to another by chemicals called neurotransmitters. Studies have found that depressed people have lower levels of certain chemicals in their brain. Medication works in some people by increasing the amount of chemicals available for use by the brain at any one time. Though accepting medication made me feel I had failed even more as a Christian, there was nothing left for me to do. I agreed to try.*

---

*For an excellent discussion on medication and other options for treating depression, see The Masks of Melancholy by John White, Inter-Varsity Press, 1982.

CHAPTER FOUR
Letting Go

My life is cold and dark and dreary;
It rains, and the wind is never weary;
My thoughts still cling to the moldering past
But the hopes of youth fall thick in the blast,
And the days are dark and dreary.

~ Henry W. Longfellow

T he medication worked well. I was soon out of the darkness and unable to understand how I got there in the first place. I didn't refill the prescription for the third course.

For a while, life went on as though nothing had happened. I refused to recognize the part that medication had played in my improvement, believing I had finally pulled myself together sufficiently to earn help from Jesus.

I still held to the lie that life was a continuing struggle to perform well enough to become acceptable to Him. The truth is that all who believe in Jesus are already acceptable through the cross by faith. Our works are of no value in reaching out to Him. The best part of being a Christian is learning to rest in the fact that we are His "pearl of great price." He gave all He had to redeem us, and nothing will ever separate us from His love.

୫ର

The children were in school by this time and I was discovering that they were indeed unique individuals. I remember well the time Jason came home and insisted they had a rodeo at school that day. When I queried him further, I learned Ruth's first grade teacher had demanded that she eat her sandwich before her cookie. Ruth threw a violent temper tantrum that took four teachers to control. I was horrified at her lack of respect for authority. She was angry about their abuse of authority and unfairness. Her outrage with injustice continued to cause trouble for her, both in and out of school. She always defended the "underdogs." As a result, she often took the anger directed at them upon herself. Today, she still maintains a strong sense of justice. It's one of the many things I love about her.

As the children got into middle school, their problems seemed to escalate. Jason was quick and bright, and often bored in school. He tended to get into trouble unless an understanding teacher kept him motivated. When he felt a teacher didn't care, he refused to cooperate, but would either cut class or disrupt it and end up in the principal's office. The school called almost daily. I often joked that I never answered the phone "Hello," anymore; I just said, "What has he done now?"

Jason and I seemed to lock horns much of the time. Though most children know their limits and will stop when they get you to the edge, this child seemed to delight in pushing me over. My illness was still undiagnosed and I was often in an extreme state of depression or agitation that left me barely able to function. The energy just wasn't there to handle a strong-willed young man. As a result, I wasn't always consistent or fair, but often either too harsh or too indulgent. At the time, I was doing the best I could. I praise God that He can both forgive my failings and repair any wounds I left in my son. Today, Jason's quick wit and hilarious sense of humor are among his most endearing traits, but as a child, his teachers and I didn't always find him funny.

When I went to pick him up from middle school one day, a secretary verbally attacked me in the parking lot. "Your son is the worst brat I've ever seen. The little monster needs to be beaten!" She raved on about what a horrible child Jason was. I was angry until I learned what had happened. Jason had been sent to the office again, and because all their isolation rooms were full, they placed him in the vice-principal's office. Using the phone at the desk, he had called that poor woman all day long asking, "Is your refrigerator running? Then you'd better go catch it." She had been beside herself all afternoon, but couldn't turn the phone off, as it was the main line. How someone else could have rung through on that line is anybody's guess.

γ_∂

Jason tended to associate with kids a lot older than himself. They seemed okay for the most part, but I think he was exposed to many things that destroyed the innocence that should have remained with him longer. A born leader, Jason soon was president of every club he joined. He often formed clubs and rallied other kids around him. We saw such great potential for God in this strong personality.

Ruth was highly independent. Though she didn't openly antagonize her teachers, she had a very difficult time socially—especially as she got to the preteen years. She didn't care to dress and act like the other girls, and had a sensitive nature and strong sense of justice that kept her from joining attacks on the unpopular students. Instead, she became their advocate, standing with them against the crowd. She was soon ostracized by the "ruling class," and was spit on, hit, pushed, and generally bullied. One student chalked, "Ruth is a DOG!" on the blackboard. The teacher never bothered to erase it, but left it on the board the entire hour. Momma went to school over that one! It didn't happen a second time.

Ruth joined Child Evangelism Fellowship (CEF) during this time and found she had a real gift for leading children to Christ. She enjoyed the recognition of doing something well, and she enjoyed working with children. We were so proud as we watched her gifts being used for God. The problems at school, however, continued to plague her. She became ill and had to drop out of CEF—just when she had been appointed the leader for her area. The church youth group kept their distance, also. Ruth had few friends. It all proved too much for a young teenager. She lost interest in everything and joined a group that every high school has: the clique of the untouchables, the unacceptable, the group with no rules of conduct, in which everyone is accepted simply because they are accepted nowhere else.

Steve and I couldn't understand what more we could have done. We had prayed for and with these children all their lives. We had envisioned that, like us, they would find Jesus at a young age and appropriate His Truth and Power to get along in the world and withstand peer pressure. When we brought our newborn children home from the hospital, I immediately set them on my lap and told them in simple words how Jesus loved them. We wanted them to hear the story from the very beginning.

We thought they would sail through life with only minor problems. Now Jason was bored, unhappy, and becoming a discipline problem, while Ruth was running with a crowd that had no standards or principles. They both absolutely refused to attend church, and the church didn't know how to reach out to them. In fact, the youth group rejected them. The situation left both of us scratching our heads in confusion. I remained in a state of deep depression through most of their school years.

৵

Things improved a little for Jason in high school. On his second day as a freshman, I received a call from the vice-principal. It was starting all over again and I almost cried—until I heard her telling me how bright Jason was. She wanted to move him into the college prep courses to challenge him more. Finally, someone had recognized the problem!

Jason also discovered debate, something he had been practicing on his parents since he was two years old. He was very good at it! He won many awards and trophies, and his debate coach remains a friend of his even now, many years later. Jason was quite active (nose tackle on the football team) and very independent. He still had trouble getting along with some teachers and counselors, though his fun sense of humor carried him much of the time.

He could be both ingenious and persuasive when he wanted something. One day he arrived home early, telling me he had been excused to do "research." He had a hall pass that said he had to leave "for a meeting at the White

House." Every teacher had signed it and he had come home. Jason graduated early after completing his junior year. Having been accepted at several colleges, he chose George Washington University in Washington, D.C.

Ruth continued with the dangerous crowd she had become a part of, though we tried everything to redirect her. She eventually suffered a breakdown while in high school. She was hospitalized for a time, and diagnosed with bipolar disorder. She kept up with her schoolwork, but refused to go back to classes. Because she was so bright, and so resistant to continuing in school, the district allowed her to graduate as a junior, also. She had completed all the required course work, anyway. Ruth went to live with my sister in California, hoping to start over.

I knew it was time to let them go, but I couldn't allow my dreams to be completely shattered. I had planned for them to leave my home as Christians, completely sold out to the Lordship of Jesus Christ. It tore my heart out to see them leave before I saw the fruit of my dream. One day, as I prayed for them, I broke into tears. The Lord asked me a simple question. "Nancy, have I ever been unfaithful to you?"

Of course not! I thought. Many times I had waited for an answer until my patience wore thin; but He had never forsaken me. He was forever faithful!

"No, Lord!" I answered, "Never!"

He replied with the sweetest words a mother could hear: "I will never be unfaithful to your children, either."

They had been dedicated to Him from the womb and He would see that the work begun in them was completed. He wanted to see it accomplished even more than I did.

CHAPTER FIVE
Let Me Die

There are many kinds of pain
That find their mark in man.
In number they are countless,
Like Proverbs' "grains of sand."
Spirit, mind, and body, in torment oft abide,
As Satan's imps with pleasure, our comfiture deride.

~ Steven Hagerman

Though I knew that God would never fail my children, I believed I had. It had been my goal to raise two perfect children who were completely mature Christians by the time they were eighteen years old. It was a ridiculous ambition, since I was much older and had not yet reached perfection myself! When they made the usual mistakes and blunders of normal adolescents, I failed to recognize these as good learning experiences. Instead, I focused on the idea that I had somehow let them down. Because of my self-reproach, I began to rescue them from natural consequences and the cycle of codependency continued. I thank God for His faithfulness to my kids, despite my shortcomings as a mother. None of us are total failures.

My illness caused me to become self-absorbed. Just like a small child, the universe revolved around me. Everything bad that happened was my fault and I accepted responsibility for it. My days became defined by less pain or more pain.

It is hard to explain the agony of depression to someone who has never experienced it. The opposite of depression is not happiness, but hope. For me, depression was characterized by complete hopelessness. It seemed as though the pain would go on forever and nothing would ever make it better. Sometimes I wandered through the darkness of depression for weeks or even months, wallowing in the "guilt" of my assumed failures. Alternately, I got angry and hostile, not wanting to be "bothered" by anyone. Often I didn't understand what was going on and wanted someone to help me.

Perhaps a few of my journal entries from that period will communicate the depth of my pain and irrational thinking.

> *March 5: Father, I am sad and overwhelmed. I don't know why. PLEASE deliver me. Help me change my thought patterns to joy.*

> *March 9: I do not know what is wrong. I feel so ANGRY! Father, cleanse me. Take away this feeling of being overwhelmed and help me cope one day at a time.*

> *March 11: Help me to look up. I am very angry and negative. I don't know why. I'm afraid of another depression.*

I addressed this lengthy journal entry to God on July 18, 1986:

> *I have been miserable for a month or more. I am so tired of it. I want to be cheerful and happy in my soul and to delight in You, my family, and this world, but all I feel is emptiness and numbness. There's a metal case around my heart and sometimes I wonder—will I ever feel again? Lord I do believe You care about me. I want my flesh to be put to death. I long for You to have my life, to shine through me. But all I feel is this aching hollow dullness. It seems so long since there has been any happiness. Is this physical? I've been prayed with, anointed, counseled and still the ache is there. Where is JOY? A black cloud engulfs me. I'm sorry I've been so self-centered. Please forgive me.*

የ&

The relationship with my husband was suffering. We went for marriage counseling, which helped short-term. The problem stemmed from my feelings of being unlovable and unlovely, and that was not his fault. I was in the habit of believing most of the lies that darted through my mind and my as-yet-undiagnosed chemical imbalance left me without energy to resist.

Steve found it harder to come home in the evening, because he never knew what he was coming home to. Sometimes I was agitated, restless, and hostile toward him. I was unable to sit down, talked incessantly, spent money we didn't have, and became highly critical of anything he did. More often, he would return home to find me wallowing in a pit of despair, TV dinners on the table and a cluttered house. In my confused state of mind, I "knew" I was unlovable and that he was only there because he was a Christian. He could not go back on his commitment to me. At the same time, I resented him because I still wanted his love but would not allow myself to accept it. Any gestures he made were dismissed because I firmly believed he was only acting. There was nothing he could have done that would have convinced me otherwise as long as my mind was so full of deception.

He tells me now that he turned to the Lord often in those days. He just didn't know how much more he could take. But he remained faithful and committed. He is a hero to me today, and a living example of Christ's love for His bride, the Church.

I realize how privileged I was to have the support of a man like Steve. Many of you have partners who are not able to be so supportive. Those still living in the pain may not realize how sympathetic your spouse really is. Please don't discount the love of God for you at this point. My husband was there for me because of God's love for both of us. If God doesn't find anyone immediately available whom He can use to pour His love through, He can shower you with it directly. There is absolutely nothing, including depression or lack of support, which can separate you from the love God holds for you. Trust Him and He will create a great waterfall of His love, gushing directly into your heart. I know He can, because He did it for me. It took a lot of healing before I could realize all He'd done.

❧

Shortly before Steve and I learned that an actual illness was causing my problems, I began to experience frightening symptoms. It is still easy to recall the terror I felt the first time I got lost. I was driving on one of the busiest streets in town when a red light stopped me. As I sat and waited, I suddenly realized that nothing looked familiar to me. It was like being somewhere I had never been before. Even worse, I could not remember where I was going or how to get back home. The light changed and I continued straight ahead, crying and not knowing what to do. Before long, the way home came to me as quickly as it had been forgotten, and once there I stayed put. I never did remember where I was going. No real harm was done, but it took a long time for the panic to subside.

I found I could no longer remember where the stamp went on an envelope! If Steve wasn't around to ask, I had to dig through the trash to find a used envelope to copy. It was months before I could remember which toothbrush was mine. Every morning I would carry both of them in to my husband, who would identify mine. Sometimes, I would forget again before I got back to the bathroom.

Names were hard to keep in mind. I was terribly embarrassed when I tried to introduce my best friend and couldn't remember her name. When I did venture out to shop, I could never find my car when I came back out, and would spend hours walking up and down the lanes searching for it. I was thoroughly humiliated, when a sack boy accompanied me outside and I had to confess I had no idea where I was parked.

I couldn't remember how old I was or when I was born. Well-known phone numbers disappeared from my memory. During this period all the routine, mechanical items stored in memory for easy recall were gone. My brain had shut down. I was terrified.

We went to several doctors who could not diagnose the problem. Some thought it was a brain tumor, others suspected multiple sclerosis, but all my tests came back normal. Steve finally made an appointment with the psychiatrist who had diagnosed me with depression seventeen years earlier. He insisted that, this time, he was coming with me.

Steve knew that in my answers to the doctors I always tried to cover up my problems. I was afraid they would diagnose me as insane. With Steve present in the office, every time I downplayed a symptom, he would gently correct me. The doctor finally got a complete picture of what was going on. He diagnosed me as bipolar and started me on Lithium, a drug that helps level extreme mood swings. He also prescribed an anti-depressant. I hated the idea of medication, but was so desperate by this time that I was willing to try anything.

҉

Things began looking up a little, though the memory problems still troubled me for a while. The doctor had warned me to avoid stress, because it tends to aggravate the symptoms of manic-depressive illness. I was trying hard to follow his instructions, when we received a call from our daughter who was living in California. She'd been asked to move out of the room she was renting and had spent the previous night in her car. That morning, some boys had taken her car without permission while she was at work, and totaled it in the desert. Within two hours, I was on the road. So much for avoiding stress!

It was a sixteen-hour trip and I drove straight through. I picked her up, dealt with the car, and returned home the next day. We hoped she had learned something about choosing her friends wisely.

In the meantime, our son had joined a fraternity and became the youngest president they ever had. His grades that year dropped far below the average necessary to maintain his scholarship. When he came to us for help, I was the one to tell him to get a loan. He learned a good lesson about priorities and responsibility. But, because I believed I had to buy his love with my behavior, I felt I had failed as a mother again.

In spite of our hopes, Ruth took up with the same crowd of friends she had been with through high school. It wasn't long after her return home that she sat me down, brought me a cup of tea, choked on a sob, and informed me she was pregnant. She was eighteen years old.

The father of the baby was not supportive, except to offer her an abortion. His mother was the director of the local abortion clinic and had it all arranged. Along with friends, I had picketed that clinic for years. I'd often locked eyes with the director as I knelt on the sidewalk out front and prayed for the babies, their mothers, and the clinic staff. Little did I suspect that one day, this woman would threaten the life of my first grandchild. I still pray that one day, God will open her eyes and that she might find forgiveness in Him.

Thank God, Ruth did not buy into the current deception. Abortion is not a simple, easy procedure that hurts no one. She couldn't compound the wrong that had already been done with an act of violence against an innocent child. Praise God! Steve and I wouldn't exchange our precious little granddaughter for all the treasure in the world.

Having an abortion often scars a woman physically and/or emotionally for the rest of her life. It wounds the mother, kills the baby, and our whole society is deprived of the special person God brought into being for His own unique purposes. If you are among the many women who have experienced abortion, my words are not meant to cause pain or make you feel guilty. I pray you will reach out to Jesus for the comfort, healing, and love He has for you. You are so precious to Him!

⸙

When Ruth stood adamantly against the abortion, her young man declared he wasn't the father, anyway, and left. It was devastating at the time.

I have never seen anyone sicker during pregnancy than Ruth. She experienced "morning, noon, and night sickness" for nine months. We took to carrying quart-sized cups in all our vehicles so we wouldn't have to pull over quite so often. She lost weight and the doctor became concerned. The baby rolled into a breech position. Ruth's pregnancy was fast becoming high-risk.

The baby was not due until the end of October, so when Steve was invited to do a three-week speaking tour in the Pacific Northwest that September, he agreed. Reluctantly, I helped him pack and very grudgingly said good-bye. I was still quite near the end of my rope and needed a lot of support. I feared I might crash completely with him gone.

That day, Ruth scrubbed the nursery area until it sparkled and sorted the baby clothes yet again. Because I had always gone on a cleaning frenzy just before entering labor, her activities made me sit up and take notice. But the baby was not due for almost six weeks. It was too early for her to be in labor.

The evening Steve left, Ruth informed me she was having some cramps. I told her it was most likely false contractions, and if she took a warm bath and relaxed, she'd probably be fine.

The next morning she was still having mild cramps, so I suggested a brief walk. Her pregnancy book said that a short walk would often cause false labor pains to go away. We hadn't gone very far before it became quite apparent this was **not** false labor. It was definitely the real thing. I half-carried and half-dragged her back to the car and we raced to the hospital. When we arrived, Ruth was in the late stages of labor. It was too late to stop it. Ready or not, I was going to be a grandmother that very day!

CHAPTER SIX

Hospitalization

Defeat may serve as well as victory
To shake the soul and let the glory out.
When the great oak is straining in the wind,
The boughs drink in new beauty and the trunk
Sends down a deeper root on the windward side.
Only the soul that knows mighty grief
Can know the mighty rapture. Sorrows come
To stretch out spaces in the heart for joy.

~ Edwin Markham

Ruth's doctor had given her exercises to do in hopes that the baby would move out of the breech position. At a routine visit two days earlier, we learned that she had turned. We thought everything would be fine.

While the nurses readied Ruth for delivery, they discovered that the little one had turned once more. She was again breeched and the umbilical cord was wrapped tightly around her neck. An emergency c-section was arranged and the hospital allowed me to accompany Ruth into surgery. I watched and prayed as the doctor struggled to slip a finger between the baby's neck and the cord that choked her. How we rejoiced when it was finally tied off and cut! Adrienne was whisked away for immediate attention from a pediatrician while the doctor finished with Ruth.

It was one of the high points of my life when that little girl, whom Satan had tried so hard to deprive the world of, was placed in my arms. With five tiny, perfect fingers wrapped around one of mine, and a look from those beautiful blue eyes, she captured my heart.

Adrienne would spend nine days in the neo-natal intensive care unit. She weighed only a little over four pounds and wasn't ready to make it on her own. She needed to be fed every two hours. Ruth had chosen to breast-feed, which worked well while they were both in the hospital, but turned into an absolute nightmare when Ruth returned home. They'd dismissed her after three days, but she wanted to make sure the baby was being held regularly, so we returned every two hours for the baby's feedings.

The drive to and from our home took about twenty minutes. By the time we arrived at the hospital, found a parking space, fed the baby, and returned home, it was almost time to go back again. Ruth was only four days out of surgery, and within a couple of days, she was totally exhausted. She tried hard to keep up with the feedings but by the second evening, collapsed onto the couch.

Sometimes, especially in periods of stress, we fail to really notice our loved ones. But something in the way she fell onto the sofa that night caught my attention. Her cheeks were flushed and her knees were drawn up as if she were in pain. When I checked her incision, it was red and angry-looking and her temperature was 103 degrees Fahrenheit. We rushed to the emergency room to discover she had developed a severe infection in her incision and was very ill. They treated her with antibiotics and sent her home. The next morning she stepped into the shower and hemorrhaged.

The doctor stabilized her and gave instructions for complete bed rest. She was to continue with her antibiotic and one additional drug, both to be taken every four hours around the clock. She was not to lift more than one pound. We both believed it was important that Adrienne be held a lot, so I continued the two-hour schedule by myself, taking Ruth's milk to the hospital in sterile containers.

Adrienne was finally able to come home and I borrowed a wheelchair so Ruth could go with me to pick her up. She weighed just four pounds, three ounces, and looked like a tiny doll when we rolled out the door with her.

By this time, I was beginning to feel the sleep deprivation, and the moodiness and mental confusion were returning. The stress didn't recede with the baby at home. While she had remained in the hospital, the nurses had taken care of her feedings every two hours at night, but now it was up to us, and Ruth couldn't lift her. I set my alarm to go off at two hours through the night and got up with the baby. I let Ruth sleep through every other feeding, trying to help her regain her strength. I couldn't nap during the day because of the home sewing business I'd operated for years. The dry cleaning service and department stores I'd contracted with needed their work done on time.

Looking back, I wish I had asked for help. I could have gone to my church friends, or my mother, or even called Steve to come home—but I didn't. My life's main operating principle was still to earn my worth. Performing well was the only way I could buy both my family's and God's approval and love. To ask for help was to lose my chance to earn respect and perhaps to finally become "good enough." It was only a few days before "Mrs. Invincible" completely crashed.

ℰ

That morning, I couldn't remember my name. It felt like things were crawling on me, and though I brushed at them, I couldn't get them off. I cried as I tried to get dressed, because the decision of what to wear was too much for me to handle. My brain just wouldn't work. The worst symptom was the all-encompassing panic. I knew "they" were going to get me, but I had no idea who "they" were, or what I had done. My mouth was dry and I was beginning to hyperventilate. From deep inside, I could feel screams rising and I didn't know if I could control them. I felt as though I might start running wildly through the streets, tearing my hair and shrieking. My body didn't seem like it was mine any longer. Somehow, I managed to get a nurse to come to stay with Ruth, called Steve to come home, and asked a friend to take me to the hospital.

It seemed an eternity as I sat waiting in the emergency room. I was afraid I would begin screaming louder and louder and not be able to stop. One of my greatest fears is losing control of myself, and I knew I was very close to losing it! Remaining still was impossible. I paced continually, wringing my hands, or swinging my arms in wide arcs. The doctor spent only a few minutes with me before he sent me upstairs.

The first thing I noticed was that they locked the door behind me when I arrived on the third floor. They took my socks and shoes, wedding ring, and watch, and stored them in a locker. I was allowed nothing except a T-shirt, sweatpants, and underwear. No buttons, zippers, or anything I could possibly hurt myself with was permitted. Combs, toothbrushes, and toiletries were all stored at the nurse's station to be checked out when I needed them. They had to be promptly returned. It wasn't fun, but it was safe, and safe was what I needed right then. I prayed they could make me well.

Hospital personnel gave me lists of words describing feelings and asked me to circle the ones I identified with. The words give a picture of my soul at the time.

> *Anxious, ashamed, crushed, defeated, edgy, empty, fearful, guilty, ignored, lonely, restless, sorry, and weepy.*

It breaks my heart to look at the list now and realize that at the time, although I was a child of God, entitled to all the rights and privileges of His Kingdom, I ignored them and chose to believe Satan's lies. One of the most important exercises I did while hospitalized was to make a list of the five most negative beliefs I held about myself. These were referred to as "Primal Law," the operating system within one's life that all thoughts and beliefs are based upon. I was then asked to list positive alternatives to replace them. They referred to this as "Eternal Law." I called it *Truth*.

This exercise was such a watershed in my life that I've included a whole chapter later in this book on the principle of telling yourself the truth. The five original "Primal Laws" I recorded are listed below, along with the Scripture verses I applied as truth. The initials PM designate Primal Law. Eternal Law has a T.

1. (PM) I am unattractive.

   (T) *So God created man in His own image...
   God saw all that He had made, and it was very
   good* (Genesis 1:27,31).

2. (PM) If I do enough people will love me.

   (T) *Martha, Martha,...you are worried and upset
   about many things, but only one thing is needed.
   Mary has chosen what is better, and it will not be
   taken away from her* (Luke 10:41,42).

3. (PM) One should be thoroughly competent, adequate, and accomplished in all respects.

   (T) *For He knows how we are formed; He
   remembers that we are dust* (Psalm 103:14).

4. (PM) One should have perfect control over things, especially oneself.

   (T) *If we claim to be without sin, we deceive
   ourselves...* (1 John 1:8).

5. (PM) If I am not responsible all the time, then I will fail the ones I love the most.

   (T) *Can a mother forget the baby at her
   breast?... Though she may forget, I will not forget you! I have engraved you on the palms of my
   hands* (Isaiah 49:15,16).

While I worked on negative thinking and other ways I contributed to my depression, the doctors were simultaneously trying to regulate my brain chemistry with medication. They explained that bipolar illness was caused by a chemical imbalance in the brain in the same way that many other illnesses are caused by an imbalance in different parts of the body. The mood swings and odd behavior were not my fault. Manic-depression was an illness that needed medication. I didn't resist anymore. The breakdown and panic attack had left me exhausted and scared out of my wits. I wanted to be well and I didn't care what it took.

Finding the right medication and correct dosage was harder than it sounded. There were times I felt so much energy, I could hardly stand myself. I'd call family members to share grandiose plans that made no sense, or corner other patients, talking incessantly, and fiddling with the curtains or any thing else I could get my hands on. At those times, I'd pace the floors and beg to be allowed to stay up past curfew because I could not settle down and stay in bed.

By contrast, there were times when the nurses had to almost drag me from my room for meetings or meals. I wanted to hide from everyone and cried much of the time. Life seemed a cruel joke for the first weeks, but eventually, as the doctors tried different medications and dosages, I began to level out. The time was coming when I would have to rejoin the world.

༄

The first time my husband obtained a pass to take me out of the hospital for dinner, I was as nervous as a teenager on a first date. My self-esteem was completely shot and I was unsure of myself. My husband had promised to care for me in "sickness and health," but neither of us had considered mental illness.

I wondered if he still really loved me or if he felt sorry for me. Would he decide to remain with me out of pity? Or would he leave because there was no enjoyment in being around me anymore? I knew that I wasn't always fun, and sometimes really difficult, to be around. I considered asking the doctor to relay a message that I couldn't see him, but I knew the meeting could not be postponed forever. I was waiting when he arrived.

Before long, we were eating and visiting like the old married couple we were. What can be better than finding out someone loves you for who you are rather than how much you do? It didn't matter to Steve that I had broken down. He only wanted to see me well and happy and was committed to staying by my side for the rest of my life. How could I not get well with a fan like that?

My daughter began bringing my precious granddaughter to visit and cheer me up. Everyone in the ward would gather round her, cooing and making silly faces in a contest to see who could make the baby smile first. *She* didn't care where Grandma was. She just enjoyed seeing me.

I was getting well. The medications had stabilized me and I was learning to take control of my thought life. Though I was frightened at the idea of going home, the love and encouragement of friends and family surrounded me and I soon left the hospital.

Things went well for a long time—until a doctor who didn't know me decided that I should quit my medicines cold turkey. Foolishly, without consulting my psychiatrist, I did. Within forty-eight hours, I completely crashed. The downward spiral continued for about two weeks, until I no longer had any desire to live. That was the Sunday morning I sat at breakfast with my husband and declared that I could bear my life no longer! I would never make it out of the pit on my own, and I knew I wasn't worthy of God's help. I prayed to die.

I went to church that morning because I couldn't face being alone. It was during the morning prayer time that the pastor's wife began relating my feelings, using the very same words I had spoken privately that morning. Then she gave me a message from God: He was not just reaching out to me, but had actually climbed into the pit with me to help me out. I decided Satan would not have me this time. I was not going down without a fight!

Part II
The Solid Rock

This I recall to my mind,
Therefore I have hope.
The Lord's lovingkindnesses indeed never cease,
For His compassions never fail.
They are new every morning;
Great is Thy faithfulness.
"The Lord is my portion," says my soul,
"Therefore I have hope in Him."

~ Lamentations 3:21-24 (NASV) ~

CHAPTER SEVEN
Help Me Fight

Blessed be the Lord, my rock,
Who trains my hands for war,
And my fingers for battle;
My lovingkindness and my fortress,
My stronghold and my deliverer;
My shield and He in whom I take refuge....

~ Psalm 144:1,2 (NASV)

I have a doll that belonged to my mother seventy years ago. She has genuine human hair in a lovely auburn color that matched my mother's. Her dress was lovingly made by my grandmother, with tiny pin tucks all sewn by hand. The shoes are leather—cut and sewn by my great grandfather Gann, who was crippled, and pieced quilts as well as doing leatherwork to support his family.

I think the doll is beautiful, but she has large cracks all over her face and body, put there by time and neglect. One day, I took her to a friend's doll shop to see what could be done about restoring her. It was bad news. There was just too much damage and the head would have to be replaced. That would never do. I wanted the doll in her original form, not a remade one, no matter how stylish. My friend told me that if I made a thin solution of glue and water and rubbed it on, it might fill some of the cracks. I took her home and tried it. The glue helped a little but she'll never be beautiful to anyone but me.

Wouldn't it be wonderful if there were a way to keep the entire doll complete and still restore her to her original state? Not to simply refurbish her so that she looks better, but to renew her completely. I wonder if God had thoughts along that line as He watched Adam and Eve leave the garden while the tears ran down His cheeks.

God had created man exactly as He intended him to be. Genesis 1:26-29 gives us a picture of man's high position before his fall from grace.

> Then God said, "Let us make man in our image, in our likeness; and let them **rule over** the fish of the sea and the birds of the air, **over** the livestock, **over** all the earth, and **over** all the creatures that move along the ground. So God created man in His own image...male and female He created them. God blessed them and said to them, "Be fruitful and increase in number; fill the earth and subdue it. **Rule over** the fish of the sea and the birds of the air and over every living creature that moves on the ground." Then God said, "I **give** you every seed-bearing plant on the face of the whole earth and **every tree** that has fruit with seed in it. They will be yours for food."

I have highlighted the words that refer to authority or ownership in the above quote. Adam was master of all he surveyed. He walked and talked with the Creator of the universe, daily, on an intimate basis. He had the companionship and love of a family, all the food he could want, useful work to do, and peaceful serenity and beauty all around him. The Father provided a perfect environment for him before he was ever created. Adam had it all, just as God had planned. His was the most fulfilling life imaginable, and God furnished him with a powerful tool to help him keep it that way. That tool was—**authority.**

As we look at the above verse again, we find that Adam had authority to rule over all the cattle and every creeping thing that creeps on the earth. This included the serpent. Though the serpent was craftier than any other beast God had made, there was still a chain of authority, and the serpent was on the bottom. A diagram of that chain, before man's fall, would look like this:

GOD
⇩
MAN
⇩

FISH ⇦   ⇨BIRDS⇦   ⇨BEASTS (SERPENT) ⇦   ⇨CREEPING THINGS

God handed the reins of power to Adam in the beginning. He was the crown of creation and the Father had only the best in mind for him from the very first on through eternity.

The account of creation and the fall of man are found in the first book of the Bible, Genesis 1-3. From the biblical text we understand that the Tree of the Knowledge of Good and Evil stood in the Garden of Eden and was the one thing not given to Adam. In fact, God commanded him not to eat of it.

Adam disobeyed his Father's direct order. The serpent tempted Eve first, then Adam through her, and both sin and death entered the world. Adam had been given complete authority over the serpent. He could have chosen to curse him as God did later on, but he didn't.

How different things would be today if Adam, instead of accepting the fruit, had said,

> *because you have done this, cursed are you above all the livestock and all the wild animals! You will crawl on your belly and you will eat dust all the days of your life* (Genesis 3:14).

Adam had power over the serpent. He could have done it. Nevertheless, he chose not to, and the world has been cursed with sin and death ever since.

Many of us are taught in Sunday School that "Jesus died for our sins so that we can go to heaven." That is very true, but it's not complete. There is so much more, and it is only when we begin to appreciate this fact that we begin to understand how to fight!

When Adam didn't use his God-given authority to rule over the serpent, he handed that authority to the serpent. Sin and Death were ushered into the world and man fell from the high position the Father had intended for him. Satan had usurped man's place and now the Bible refers to him as: *the god of this age*, (2 Corinthians 4:4), *the prince of this world*, (John 14:30), and the *ruler of the kingdom of the air* (Ephesians 2:2). The diagram after the fall looks like this:

GOD

⇩

SATAN-SERPENT (SIN, DEATH)

⇩

MAN

⇩

FISH ⇐   ⇨BIRDS⇐   ⇨BEASTS⇐   ⇨CREEPING THINGS

Man could never recapture the lost ground on his own. Innocence had been destroyed, and authority set aside. Evil had entered the heart of man and was there to stay—despite the fact that we are still created in the image of God. When we see children hurt, friends betrayed, or innocence abused, it disturbs us, because His image is stamped on us. He is a God of both justice and mercy. I believe He wept as his children fled from the garden. Justice was served, but His heart of mercy had already designed a plan for restoration.

Jesus did not visit earth merely to allow us to enter heaven one day. That alone is more than we have a right to hope for, but we so easily underestimate the love God has for each of us. Jesus came to save us not only from Death but also from Sin (Romans 8:2). He came to take the curse of both upon Himself so we can again be restored to our original state. He came because God longed to reinstate us to fellowship with Him. He wanted to return all we had lost, everything He had meant for us to have.

Like the father of the prodigal son in Luke 15, He yearned to put His robe of righteousness around us and His ring of authority and restored nobility on our fingers. Just like the father who made sure sandals were brought for his son because only slaves went barefoot, He wants to eliminate any doubt about full restoration to the family. The "prodigal son" was welcomed wholeheartedly, kissed, clothed, fed, reclaimed as a son, and granted authority to use in his father's name.

We are no longer slaves to Satan and Sin. If we believe and receive Christ, we are granted the right to become children of God (John 1:12). We are no longer under Satan's power, but instead, we are given authority over him. We stand clothed in the righteousness of Christ, while all heaven rejoices at our restoration. There are still choices to make because we live in a fallen world, but we are no longer slaves to sin. We now have freedom to make those choices. When we become children of God, the diagram changes to look like this:

GOD
⇩
MAN
⇩
SATAN-SERPENT
⇩
FISH ⇦　⇨BIRDS⇦　⇨BEASTS⇦　⇨CREEPING THINGS

We must learn to stand and fight or Satan will continue to deceive us, causing us to believe we are still under his power. Imagine yourself wrapped in heavy chains padlocked together. Now, imagine Jesus unlocking the padlock and loosing the chains. If Satan can delude you into believing that the padlock is still there, you will keep on behaving as though you're bound, even though Jesus has set you free. This is where the spiritual battle begins. We must choose to believe our Lord in spite of outside circumstances or inner turmoil. The truth is—we have been set free and that's all there is to it!

God has not left us on our own in the conflict, but has granted all the protection and authority we require. As we trust and believe Jesus' promises, He will be faithful to lead us into battle. Psalm 18:34 promises: *He trains my hands for battle; my arms can bend a bow of bronze.* Just like Superman!

Don't get discouraged when you fail. Praise Him for picking you up, and try again. Mother Teresa was so right when she said, "The Lord never talked about success, He only talked about being faithful."

CHAPTER EIGHT

The Battle Joined

As true as God's own promise stands,
Not earth or hell with all their bands
Against us shall prevail;
The Lord shall mock them from His throne;
God is with us; we are His own;
Our victory cannot fail!

~ Gustavus Adolphus

During my battle with bipolar illness, I was in a fight for both my mind and my life against the powers of darkness. Though I still continue to struggle at times, Jesus has taught me a number of things about spiritual warfare. I've experienced much healing and learned a great deal. Some of those lessons are listed below and in the following two chapters.

1) *Remember, God loves you!* This is absolutely essential to getting well. It is your lifeline. Hang on to this simple truth.

Do whatever it takes to keep this fact foremost in your mind. Satan will try to convince you that God does not care, that you are alone in the universe, and that you've failed Him so often that you are beneath His notice. THESE ARE ALL LIES!

If you are a child of God, Satan has no power to change that fact. He has no dominion over you, because Jesus has set you free. All he can do is toss lies your way and hope you will believe them. He'll use any falsehood he can to get you to choose to remain in bondage rather than follow the truth. Satan has only the power God grants him. He is allowed to tempt and test, just as he did Job, but he must first receive permission from the Father. Any authority he is given comes straight from God Himself and is always filtered by His love. As you hang onto the truth about His love, temptations and trials only make you stronger.

I carry a button in my pocket that was originally passed out by a jewelry store promoting diamond rings. It simply says, "I am loved." Yes, diamonds are valuable. But this button reminds me that I am worth even more than diamonds to God. No sacrifice was too great for Him to make in order to restore our fellowship. His children are His special treasure (Exodus 19:5).

If you are not a child of God, you must know that you are without real protection against the Enemy of your soul. Only true children of God can claim the authority and power that come with being one of His. Jesus came to reinstate us to our proper position. He conquered both Sin and Death, and He is our only hope of restoration with the Father. The truth is always there: God loves you.

The Word of God tells us to believe and be saved. In Greek, the language of the New Testament, *belief* is more than just an acknowledgement of fact. It means to trust, to adhere to, and to rely on. There comes a time when each of us must realize that we cannot fix ourselves. All the good we try to do is never enough to fill the void inside. It's then that we comprehend that Jesus is our only hope. If you haven't done so, I pray that you will search for Him. As you take a small baby-step toward Him, He'll take giant leaps toward you.*

ॐ

A good illustration of someone who understands the never-ending love of God is found in the account of Joseph (Genesis 37-50). As the story begins, we find Joseph literally in the pit, where his own brothers had thrown him. He is finally lifted out, sold to Ishmaelite traders, and subsequently becomes a slave in Egypt. He is falsely accused of attempted rape by his master's wife and sent to prison. While in prison, he helps Pharaoh's cup-bearer and asks to be remembered before Pharaoh when the official is restored to his position. But again he is forgotten—by everyone but God!

Imagine how Joseph might have felt. God had given him dreams where even his father and brothers bowed down before him, but in fact, he had been either a slave or a prisoner all his adult life. Do you think he was tempted to doubt the truth that God loved him when it seemed as though every time he raised his head he was cast down again? Do you suppose he was tempted to get angry and just give up on God, or wonder if He existed at all? Joseph remained faithful because, at some time in the past, he had determined in his heart that God loved him personally and wanted only the best for him. He knew his Lord cared for him and nothing would dissuade him from that truth.

---

*For further information about how to become a child of God see Appendix I.

Joseph held on to his belief with all he had. In His appointed time, God lifted him up and all the promises came to pass.

Later on, when he had an opportunity to get even with his brothers, he simply acknowledged that, *you intended to harm me, but God intended it for good* (Genesis 50:20). It is essential, whether you are in the pit or on the mountaintop, that you never allow yourself to forget or doubt that *God loves you.*

2) *Seek medical help.* Why is it that so many Christians think nothing of taking an aspirin for a headache or insulin for diabetes, yet refuse to consider the idea of taking medication for mental illness? As mentioned earlier, most bipolar illness is caused by a chemical imbalance in the brain. Chemicals are needed to carry messages across the small gap, or synapse, between one nerve ending and another. When normal amounts of these chemicals are present, everything is fine. When the amounts are low, whatever is supposed to happen within that particular nerve transmission doesn't. If this type of deficiency takes place in the body (arms or legs for instance) loss of motion or limitations of function occur. When it takes place in the brain, the result is termed *mental illness*, even though there is a definite physical cause. Researchers don't agree on whether the imbalance is triggered by a response to stress or if a heightened response to stress is caused by the imbalance. It doesn't matter too much when you just want to get well. The reality is, the imbalance exists and needs to be dealt with.

❧

There are other illnesses that can cause symptoms of depression, both unipolar and bipolar.* It is important that your physician rule them out. Illnesses known to include symptomatic depression include: thyroid disease, diabetes, multiple sclerosis, certain vitamin deficiencies, and more.

Your doctor will probably give you a complete physical and, if indicated, will prescribe medication. There is nothing shameful or un-christian about taking prescribed medicine for your illness. When the idea was first presented to me, I felt I was being offered a crutch to limp along with because I was too weak in my faith to walk alone. I have since discovered that, when your leg is broken, it makes more sense to use a crutch while growing strong and getting well than to lie down and give up. My doctor pointed out that many people, Christians included, need insulin to regulate their blood sugar. Using medication to regulate the chemical imbalance implicated in depression is no different. Diabetes involves a chemical imbalance, too.

Don't give up if the first doctor you try is not sympathetic. There are many fine doctors out there who are quite skilled in helping with depression. Psychiatrists, especially, are trained to deal with chemical imbalance in

---

*Depression is grouped into two classes. Unipolar symptoms consist of: Feeling tired all the time, sleep disturbances, irritability, sadness and/or tears for no apparent reason, loss of sex drive, headache, lack of enthusiasm or feelings of enjoyment, inability to concentrate or make decisions, and feeling unwanted, guilty and worthless; often leading to the belief that life is not worth living. Bipolar illness has the same symptoms of depression but also includes extreme mood swings. People with these symptoms tend to swing from being happy and playful, to severely depressed—though during manic times, they tend to describe themselves as more restless and "driven" than genuinely happy. This is by no means a complete list and should not be considered a means for medical analysis. Only your physician can make the correct diagnosis with you.

the brain. Ask for referrals from your pastor or friends and pray for guidance. God wants to see you free and whole even more than you do. Don't get discouraged! Medication takes time to work, and because we all have our own unique body chemistry, a doctor may have to experiment with different dosages and kinds of medicine. It takes a while, but the time spent is well worth it

When you are in the throes of a major depression, it is almost impossible to concentrate hard enough to seek truth and healing. What your mind believes as absolute fact is not necessarily reality. The right medication can restore the normal functioning of your brain so you can begin to get well.

It is important not to stop your medication on your own, but to do so only under a doctor's care. People with bipolar illness have a reputation for stopping their medication abruptly. When you are no longer depressed, you feel you don't need it. Also, many people miss the manic episodes because of the euphoria they bring.

Stopping medication on your own is dangerous! Whenever I did in the past, besides making me physically ill for a few days, it nearly always caused me to ricochet into a worse depression than before. Commit to yourself and a friend that you will not stop your medication until you, your friend, and your doctor agree that it is time.

3) *Exercise and watch your nutrition.* This is difficult during depression. The very last thing you want is to get out of bed and do anything—particularly exercise. There were also times when I didn't care if I ate at all. Other times I ate everything in sight, especially sweets. Chocolate was my preferred choice and scientists have now discovered a reason for this. The article quoted in the next paragraph

explains it well. You can find it on the Internet at *http://www.pathmed.com/demo/id64_m.htm.*

> *Chocolate has been used to self-medicate our low moods. Because of this pseudo-elevating effect, it was once known as the food of the gods. It is derived from cocoa beans, which are fermented to rid them of their bitterness. They are then dried, cleaned and roasted to develop color, flavor and aroma. Chocolate contains phenylethylamine, known for causing emotional highs and lows associated with mood swings, love, pleasure, and indulgence. Chocolate also contains the chemical theobromine, which triggers the release of endorphins in the brain and works as a natural antidepressant. But in the long run this chemical, with continued intake, will probably deplete endorphins and will not lead to their restoration. So many drugs that enter into the addiction model, although they temporarily release good medicine into the brain, will result in depletion because they do not rebuild. Chocolate is another fermented food and therefore falls in the same category with alcohol and other fermented products, which often have negative affects on brain health.*

Most of the time when you are craving sugar, your body is really asking for simple carbohydrates like fruit and vegetables, or complex carbohydrates, such as whole grains, cereal, or pasta. These foods keep blood sugar levels constant and increase production of the chemical serotonin, which helps regulate mood. High-sugar foods like cookies and chocolate cause blood sugar levels to escalate rapidly and then crash, draining you of energy.

I find it helpful to always eat a carbohydrate and a protein together. Carbs tend to produce quicker energy and leave you feeling better faster, while proteins take longer to digest, but stay with you long-term. For a quick snack, I often try crackers and tuna salad, an apple with cheese, a handful of peanuts and raisins, or a glass of milk with a couple of graham crackers. They don't give that "wiped out" feeling like candy does and are much more satisfying.

While nutrition can help you deal with stress, exercise can actually help rid your body of that stress. Anyone who has experienced a nervous headache, or reached back to massage aching shoulder muscles, has no trouble recognizing that stress is stored in our muscles as tension. This stress can be reduced by means of exercise. Regular exercise can help stabilize moods, lower blood pressure, and improve sleep.

Exercise also raises the level of chemicals, called endorphins, in the brain. These chemicals ease pain and give a sense of well-being.

Any exercise is good for you, though my personal preference is walking. It is inexpensive, can be done almost anywhere, and the fresh air and sunshine are invaluable benefits. Exercise should not be painful. Start slowly and congratulate yourself for small victories. I began by walking ten to fifteen minutes, two or three times a day. Now I try to walk thirty minutes to one hour every day. Occasionally a day goes by when I don't walk, but that's okay. Walking has stopped being a chore and has become something special I do for myself. I feel better physically and get more done when I exercise. I've even come to look forward to it as a good opportunity for uninterrupted prayer. Walking is especially fun when done with a friend, which brings us to point number four.

4) *Find a reliable friend.* One or two good friends will prove invaluable as you work toward getting well. You can count on friends to tell you the truth when your own mind is too ill to find it. Many people don't think of their spouses in this context, but in my own search for wellness, my husband proved priceless.

There were many times when he braved my anger and hostility, while quietly and firmly telling me the truth. Because my depressions were rooted in my own sense of worthlessness and a belief that I had to earn my right to be loved, I often latched on to the belief that no one, including him, really cared for me. I would convince myself they were only being nice because they were Christians and God said they had to. My husband reassured me of his love and pointed out that God didn't have to make people be nice to me; they were nice because they liked me. When the depression became so bad that it was all I could do to get out of bed, let alone prepare supper, he either cooked or bought TV dinners. When I was so confused that I could no longer remember where the stamp went on an envelope, or what color my toothbrush was, he was always there to help me.

One of my first steps toward healing came about when I finally realized that, while in a state of depression, my own thoughts and emotions could not be trusted. I needed to trust my friends to help me interpret truth. I also promised to remain on my medication until both Steve and my doctor thought it was time for me to quit.

The Lord has used them to cut it back very gradually. Although I still take some, I have been free of most symptoms for a number of years.

If you are the spouse or friend of a depressed person, you play a very important role. Remember that your friend is ill. They truly don't see reality for what it is. It is essential that you pray for them and, as God leads, try to convince them of your love for them and their own value. There are times they won't believe you and times they may be angry and even hostile. Don't take it personally. Ask God to show you ways to help convince them of their worth to both Him and you. Small things mean a lot. Sometimes just getting out of bed is a tremendous effort for those who feel hopeless. Tell them they look nice, fix a meal, send a card, or give a hug for no reason. You may feel that nothing works, but believe me, anything you do from a spirit of love means more than you will ever know.

I leave this point with one final important note. **Take any threat of suicide very seriously!** Ask how they plan to do it. If they have a plan, you must take action. Get them to a hospital or call the police. You may save a life. If there is no definite suicide plan, they should still be taken seriously. Assume responsibility for getting them some assistance. A suicide threat is, at the least, a desperate cry for help. At most, it is a sign that the person has completely given up and is simply making a statement of fact to you. Never assume a threat of suicide is not significant.

In this chapter, we have seen how important it is to remember that God loves us, to seek medical help, to exercise and watch our nutrition, and to find reliable friends. There are two final points I want to make, and they are so vital to getting well that each warrants its own chapter.

CHAPTER NINE

Jesus is Truth

If you abide in My Word...
you shall know the truth, and
the truth shall make you free.

I am the way, and the truth, and the life....

~ Jesus (John 8:31,32; 14:6, NASV)

Telling yourself the truth is almost impossible unless you are reading the Word and praying regularly. God's Word is the only place you will find pure, authentic truth to use in countering the lies of the enemy. God will interpret and make that truth real to you as you wait on Him in prayer. He is Truth.

Psychologists have a tool available to them called "cognitive therapy." The originator is Dr. Aaron T. Beck.

Doctor Beck began to investigate then-current Freudian theories and therapies for depression, and found that, in practical application, they really didn't work very well. While his experiments didn't give support to the popular theories of the time, the data suggested a new, testable theory about the causes of emotional disturbances. The research showed that the depressed individual sees himself as a "loser," as an inadequate person doomed to frustration, deprivation, humiliation, and failure.

Further experiments revealed a marked difference between the depressed person's self-image, expectations, and ambitions on the one hand, and his actual achievements—often very striking—on the other. Beck concluded that depression must involve disturbances in the thinking of the depressed person. If the peculiar and negative ways the patient thinks about himself, his environment, and his future could be changed, he might get well.*

Dr. David Burns explains the theory in 4 points:

(1) When you are depressed or anxious, you are thinking in an illogical, negative manner, and you inadvertently act in a self-defeating way.

(2) With a little effort, you can train yourself to straighten your twisted thought patterns.

(3) As your painful symptoms are eliminated, you will become productive and happy again, and you will respect yourself.

(4) These aims can usually be accomplished in a relatively brief period of time, using straightforward methods. **

The above theory does have merit, and it has met with some success. As Christians, we need to take it another step. It is not just negative thinking patterns

---

*Feeling Good—The New Mood Therapy, David D. Burns, Signet, 1981, preface.

**Ibid., pg. 3-4

with which we wrestle, but actual lies placed in our minds by Satan. Jesus describes him in John 8:44:

> *There is no truth in him. When he lies, he speaks his native language, for he is a liar, and the father of lies.*

He whispers these lies so subtly, using our own insecurities, that we immediately accept them. We never question their validity, let alone replace them with truth. It is these very lies, when not challenged, which leave us feeling worthless, unlovable, hopeless and defeated. Is it any wonder that many years ago, Paul wrote:

> *Finally, brethren, whatever is **true**, whatever is noble, whatever is right, whatever is pure, whatever is lovely, whatever is admirable—if anything is excellent or praiseworthy—think about such things"* (Philippians 4:8, emphasis mine).

We must learn to tell ourselves the truth if we are going to be effective in this struggle for our mind. Only real truth will counter a lie. Another lie will only compound the problem.

The only way to discover genuine truth is by reading the Word of God. Jesus said,

> *if you hold to My teaching, you are really My disciples. Then you will know the **truth**, and the **truth** will set you free* (John 8:31,32, emphasis mine).

Truth can set us free from depression and from the bondage that takes place when our mental illness makes decisions for us. It can set us free to make choices based on reality rather than lies, to walk in the joy God intends for us and in fellowship with Him. God has made each of His children "a new creation." We have new hearts, renewed minds, and freedom—but we are still called to "fight the good fight of faith" as we appropriate the liberty He has granted us (1 Timothy 6:12).

The human race is only now discovering how important it is to tell yourself the truth. God knew it ages ago. The Apostle Paul addressed the issue in 2 Corinthians 10:3-5:

> For though we walk in the flesh, we do not war according to the flesh, for the weapons of our warfare are not of the flesh, but divinely powerful for the destruction of fortresses. We are destroying speculations and every lofty thing raised up against the knowledge of God, **and we are taking every thought captive to the obedience of Christ** (NASV, emphasis mine).

Paul says that, in order to wage effective spiritual warfare, we must both destroy speculations and take every thought captive. To better understand what the word *speculations* refers to, consider this list of synonyms: conjectures, assumptions, premises, theories, guesswork, hearsay, suppositions, and thoughts.

The word in Greek is *logismos,* which is derived from another Greek word that you may already be familiar with: *logos,* meaning "word." *Logismos* could be defined as *a word in your mind.* The same word is also used in Romans 2:15 where it is usually translated, *thoughts.* Speculations are assumptions, premises, theories, or "operating systems" in our psyche that come when we "hear a word in our mind" and adopt it as our own. These thoughts can come from God and be true, or from Satan and be lies. When they come from self, they can be either truth or deception.

When we assume lies are true and act on them, we set up a false belief system, both about who we are and about our relationship with God. This belief system is not rooted on a solid foundation, but built upon fabrication. We must destroy these false speculations in order to walk in freedom and wholeness. To do this, we must learn to take our thoughts captive.

Many of the thoughts we need to take captive are negative and self-condemning. Many are lies, planted in our minds by Satan in order to keep us bound and defeated. It is imperative that we learn how to listen to our thoughts and take control of them.

સ્ર

In my own quest for healing, I remember well the first time I caught myself in a lie. I'd taken a shower and happened to look into the mirror as I dried off. *Oh, Yech! You're so gross,* I thought to myself as I had done a thousand times or more. Immediately, a strong sense of conviction came over me and God spoke to my heart: *I have redeemed you; I have called you by name; you are mine! (Isaiah 43:1).* He then continued with another verse from the tenth chapter of Acts: *What God has made clean, let no man call unclean.*

Having been bought with a price—made clean by the blood of Jesus—I had no right to destroy myself by filling my mind with satanic lies. God would not tolerate His child believing this kind of garbage any longer. I literally needed to "take the trash out" of my mind, and God was going to help me. I was on my way to wholeness.

So how do we go about becoming aware of our negative thoughts, taking them captive, and replacing them with truth? First, we must ask for God's help in identifying the wrong thoughts. We also need Him to reveal the truth with which we will replace them. He alone is able to discern the true from the false, and He can bring to our minds Scriptures we can use to refute the lies. A sample prayer might go like this:

> *Thank You, Lord Jesus, for everything You did to buy my freedom. I joyfully acknowledge that freedom and am trying to walk in it. I want my mind free from deception and lies and filled up with Your Truth. I am asking You to take my thoughts captive. Bring to my consciousness the lies I have believed in the past and replace them with the Truth. Help me reject the lies as soon as I become aware of them, and fill my mind full of Truth from Your Word. I know I can always count on You to be faithful to me. Thank You for what You are preparing to do in my life. I want all You have for me. Amen*

Once we have asked for His help, we must begin to fill our minds with the Word of God. It is important to read the Bible on a regular basis. Please do not take this as a commandment; it was not listed in the original Ten! If you miss a day of reading the Word, it's okay! Try again tomorrow.

Driving yourself to read only because of strict adherence to some command authorized by Self may gain you some good. But you will also be feeding your soul on the age-old lie that good works will save you or somehow make you more acceptable to Jesus.

You are acceptable to Jesus right now, because of the blood He shed for you. No amount of Bible reading or other good deeds can earn you more grace. Jesus has already done all that's necessary, and simply wants to lavish His love and acceptance on you. He wants you to rest in that knowledge. It's important that you read, not because the "law" commands it, but because it's good for you. Reading the Word will help with your struggle to walk in freedom.

ൠ

The next thing to do is easily remembered by the anagram STOP.

S—stop
 T—thoughts
  O—on
   P—purpose

As you notice a self-condemning or negative thought cross your mind, STOP! Remind yourself that you have the right to analyze it. Hold it up to the light of God's Word and examine it. What does He say? Is it all right to tell yourself that you are dumb and ugly? Or worthless? Or unfit to be loved? Absolutely not!

God will use His Word in your mind to teach you the truth. You are far from dumb! You are extremely wise because you're trusting the Lord and not leaning toward your own understanding (Proverbs 3:5-6). Ugly? Impossible! You are fearfully and wonderfully made (Psalm

139:14). Can a child of God be worthless? Not according to the Word of God. If you were worth the precious blood of Jesus, no one, including you, has a right to label you unworthy (Hebrews 9:14). As for being unfit to be loved, read John 3:16.

> For God so loved the world, that He gave His one and only Son, that whoever believes in Him shall not perish but have eternal life.

Or Hosea 2:19-20.

> And I will betroth you to Me forever; I will betroth you in righteousness and justice, in love and compassion. I will betroth you in faithfulness, and you will acknowledge the Lord.

As you become faithful in putting the Truth into your mind, the Lord will be faithful in bringing it to mind and applying it to the lies. You will never outdo Him in faithfulness!

Some people find keeping a chart helpful in identifying negative thoughts. Separate your paper into three columns labeled, *Lies*, **Truth**, and **Bible**. Throughout the day, as you become aware of your negative self-talk, jot down all those painful self-criticisms in the *Lies* column. It is best if you can substitute a truth right away. If you can't, take some time later to record the truth in its column next to the lie. List a verse in the Bible column if you can.

LIES	TRUTH	BIBLE
I am so ugly	No! I am fearfully and wonderfully made. God thinks I'm beautiful.	Psalm 139:14
I feel so worthless	I was worth the price of Jesus' blood. He even knows my name.	Hebrews 9:14 Isaiah 43:1
No one cares	God does! I matter to Him.	1 Peter 5:7

When you first begin the exercise, you will find the lies are more easily identified. The truth may be harder to come up with. It sometimes feels "phony" or unnatural. We are not working with feelings here, but truth. The goal is to make your feelings line up with the truth, not the other way around. If you are operating from the Word, recognize that it is always true, and write it down. It will become easier as you fill your mind with truth from the Bible. As you read and your knowledge base grows, it will also become much simpler for you to list chapter and verse in the Bible column. It will be useful for you to memorize some of these verses, so that as new lies occur, the truth will be readily accessible to you.

By now, I hope you have written the fact that God loves you in indelible ink on the tablet of your mind. Have you also sought medical help, exercised and watched your nutrition, and enlisted the support of one

or two loyal friends? Are you faithfully identifying negative thoughts and replacing them with God's Word? If so,
you are probably beginning to see some success. There
remains one more thing for you to do and it is mentioned
many times in the Bible: *stand firm!*

CHAPTER TEN

Stand Firm

Soldiers of Christ, lay hold
On faith's victorious shield;
Armed with that adamant and gold,
Be sure to win the field;
If faith surround your heart,
Satan shall be subdued;
Repelled his every fiery dart,
And quenched with Jesus' blood.

Jesus hath died for you!
What can His love withstand?
Believe, hold fast your shield, and who
Shall pluck you from His hand?

~ Charles Wesley

T he first time I can remember taking a stand was in the first grade. One of the boys, who happened to be the son of a U.S. senator, informed me there was no Santa Claus and we fought. He was crying, and my mother was called. When she arrived she asked me what had happened. I replied that I had "kicked him in the stomach and told him he was A BIG, FAT LIAR." There was no repentance on my part that day. I went home in disgrace, but secretly I was proud that I had stood up for myself.

The key to standing firm is remembering that Satan is also a "big, fat liar." We already possess all the tools we need to resist him.

Ephesians 6:11-18a commands us to "stand" four times and lists for us the tools God has provided to help us do so.

> Put on the full armor of God so that you can take your **stand** against the devil's schemes. For our struggle is not against flesh and blood, but against the rulers, against the authorities, against the powers of this dark world and against the spiritual forces of evil in the heavenly realms. Therefore put on the full armor of God, so that when the day of evil comes, you may be able to **stand** your ground and after you have done everything, to **stand**. **Stand firm** then, with the belt of **truth** buckled around your waist, with the breastplate of **righteousness** in place, and with your feet fitted with the readiness that comes from the **gospel of peace**. In addition to all this, take up the shield of **faith** with which you can extinguish all the flaming arrows of the evil one. Take the helmet of **salvation**, and the sword of the spirit, which is the **Word of God**. And **pray in the Spirit** on all occasions with all kinds of prayers and requests...(emphasis mine).

We are able to take a stand and maintain it because of our confidence in the Lord Jesus. Every piece of armor we are told to put on, the Bible has already declared Jesus to be. He is:

Our **Truth** (John 14:6)
Our **Righteousness** (Jeremiah 33:16, I John 2:29)
The **Prince of Peace** (Isaiah 9:6)
The **Author of our Faith** (Hebrews 12:2)
Our **Salvation** (Hebrews 5:9, Acts 4:12)
The **Word of God** (John 1:1, Hebrews 4:12)
And He **prays** for us and with us (Romans 8:26, Hebrews 7:25)

He is everything we need. Provision is even made for the fact that we have no armor for our backs. He promises that He will not only go before us, but will be our **rear guard** (Isaiah 52:12). We can safely stand firm if we are leaning on Him.

∽

A story is told about an elderly black man who was the janitor of a school not far from a seminary. There was no gymnasium on campus, so the young men would use the public school to play basketball. The old janitor would sit patiently reading his Bible while he waited for them to finish. One day, one of the young men approached to ask what he was reading. The janitor replied, "The Book of Revelation."

The young man scoffed and wondered if he under-stood it. The old man stated confidently that he did. The youth jeered, "If you understand the Book of Revelation so well, then why don't you tell us what it means?" The old man looked him straight in the eye and answered, "It means that Jesus is gonna win!"

Don't get the idea that once you receive Jesus, there will never again be anything negative in your life. Satan is pure evil and his goal is to destroy you. One of the best illustrations of his nature comes from the book, *Perelandra*, by C.S. Lewis. In one scene, the Unman, a type of Satan, strolls through an extremely beautiful part of God's creation. The hero, following him, comes upon a trail of maimed and dying frogs. He counts over twenty along the way, until he sees the Unman about thirty feet ahead. As our hero watches, the evil being slips a fingernail under the skin at the base of the frog's skull and simply rips it open. There is only one reason for his action. The same reason that explains why he pulls the wings off of birds. He enjoys it.

Jesus warned us that Satan came to steal, kill, and destroy (John 10:10). Satan's goal is to steal our joy, kill our hope, and destroy our faith; and he will use any means at his disposal to do it. He might try immorality, confusion, discouragement, dissatisfaction, or doctrinal error. He knows where our weak points are and goes for the jugular every time. Our only hope is to take up the armor God has provided for us, and to stand firm in His name. The way to do this is to spend sufficient time in worship, prayer, and reading His Word. We need to know Him so well that we can place blind faith in Him and be assured, without a doubt, that He will see us through. Perhaps, one day, we will mature to the point that we can say with Job: *Though He slay me, yet will I trust Him.*

Spiritual warfare is not a scary, difficult thing. You don't have to take classes in order to do it right. Nor do you have to wait until you become a Super Christian. Those who are most conscious of their own weakness and inadequacy are often God's best warriors, because they are especially quick to rely on Him. To be an effective soldier in this battle, one needs only to make a choice to trust Jesus. He has already given us everything necessary for both life and godliness (1 Peter 1:3). While on the cross, Jesus cried out, "It is finished!" because that is exactly what He meant.

✿

The book of Numbers is an interesting tutorial on the subject of trust. One can read it hurriedly and still notice the many times the Israelites forgot to trust God and decided they wanted to return to slavery in Egypt.

When they were in bondage, someone else had taken care of them. Their choices were made for them—where to work, what to eat or wear, and how to act. Egypt seemed desirable because it was comfortable. They quickly forgot about the long hours, the hard work, the boring meals, and the beatings. At least they had known what to expect. Egypt was a sure thing.

By contrast, the Israelites in the wilderness had many decisions to make and responsibilities to shoulder. They were not used to being free or making choices. Every time they ran into a crisis, they wanted to go back to where they'd been comfortable. Life had been very hard in Egypt, but at least it had been familiar.

I recently received an e-mail titled, *The Biggest Mathematical Miracle in the World*. The author is unknown but what he had to say is very instructive:

> *The first crisis occurred as they were escaping: They had to get across the Red Sea in one night. If they walked on a narrow path, double file, the line would be 800 miles long and would require thirty-five days and nights to get everyone*

across. Instead, there had to be a space in the Red Sea three miles wide. They needed to walk 5,000 abreast to get across in one night. Who else but God could build a road so fast?

Once in the desert, the people had to be fed, but what was Moses going to do? Feeding two or three million people requires a lot of food. According to the Quartermaster General in the Army, Moses would have needed 1,500 tons of food each day. Delivering that much food each day would have required two freight trains, each a mile long. Nonetheless God provided them with manna every day!

Besides, you must remember, they were out in the desert and would need firewood to use in cooking the food. This would take 4,000 tons of wood and a few more freight trains, each a mile long, for just one day. The manna came fully cooked but what about the quail?

Oh, yes, they would have to have water. They needed 11 million gallons a day and a freight train of tank cars 1,800 miles long, just to bring enough water to drink and wash a few dishes! God provided water from the rocks.

And remember they were forty years in transit. Each time they camped at the end of the day, a campground two-thirds the size of the state of Rhode Island was required, or a total of 750 square miles.

Do you think Moses figured all this out before he

*left Egypt? I think not! You see, Moses believed
in God. God took care of these things for him.*

*Now, do you think God has any problem taking
care of all your needs?*

It is so easy to read through Numbers and become
smug and self-righteous. We think to ourselves, "God
would never have to discipline me for forgetting Him. I
wouldn't do that. If He held back the waters of the Red
Sea while I walked across on dry land—without even getting my shoes muddy—I would recognize His power and
trust Him for the rest of my life!"

As I sat reading Numbers one day, and feeling self-righteous about my walk with the Lord, God whispered: "You
fail to trust me almost every day." I realized then that
whenever we allow ourselves to become anxious or troubled, we are not trusting the Lord. When we fret and lose
sleep over a problem, it is because we lack faith. I began to
understand that Numbers is in the Bible to remind us that,
when we begin to worry, we have ceased to trust.

ॐ

God has promised that He will cause all things to
work together for good to those who truly love Him. He
has promised to provide all our physical needs. Jesus
told us that birds don't sow or reap or gather food into
storage, but God feeds them anyway. He then asked, *Are
you not much more valuable than they?* (Matthew.
6:26). Our God promises to protect us as He would the
pupil of His own eye! He declares that He will never fail
us nor forsake us, that all of His promises will be ful-
filled. We serve a God who is a Rock in the midst of the
storms of life.

Recall for a moment the story, told in the Gospels, of Christ calming the storm. He gets into a boat with His disciples. While they begin the trip across the lake, Jesus finds a cushion in the stern and promptly falls asleep. A fierce storm with high waves blows in. They sweep over the boat and it begins to fill up. The disciples wake Jesus and ask if He doesn't care that they are going to die. He rebukes the wind and waves, and they calm immediately. The next statement Jesus makes must be from a broken heart, especially since He is speaking to men who have been with Him continually for some time. He says, "Where is your faith?"

Let's imagine a different scenario. The storm is raging and the boat is filling with water. The disciples begin to panic until they remember who's with them. They are afraid and feel a need for His comfort, so they leave their duties and gather around Him as He sleeps. They recognize that they are with Messiah, Emmanuel, the Son of God, the Master of any storm. Joyfully they begin to praise God because they know that even if, for some reason, He allows their boat to sink and they are all drowned, they will still enjoy everlasting life in His presence for all eternity.

I realize this does not align itself with human nature. Most of us would be in absolute terror on a sinking vessel. But bear with me a few more moments while I make a point. What would Jesus' response have been when they safely reached the other side? He would definitely not have questioned their faith! I believe He would have locked eyes with each of them while He smiled, and termed them, "My Faithful Ones!" Which type of disciple would you like to be? My goal is to be *His Faithful One*.

We can also envision a different scenario for the Israelites in the wilderness. What if they had set up camp with no water or food in sight, but instead of complaining, said to one another, "I would rather remain a free child of God in the wilderness and die of starvation than return to bondage in Egypt without Him." I believe they would have still had manna and quail and water from a rock, perhaps even a steak or two! Why not? God is always faithful, even when we are faithless, although He delights in our trust.

࿓

One of the most precious things about small children is their uncomplicated trust. I love it when my granddaughters come to visit me, and I enjoy caring for them. They simply ask when they want something and expect me to provide it. In fact, I try to anticipate their needs. If they are hungry, they get a snack; if thirsty, they get a drink. If they are tired, they get a snuggle, have a book read, hear a few songs, and go to bed with their favorite blanket. (Well, I am a grandma!) The point is, they don't wring their hands and worry whether or not I will provide for their needs. They simply trust.

God, make me more like a little child that I might delight Your heart. Teach me to say with Habakkuk:

> *Though the fig tree should not bud, and there are no grapes on the vines,*
> *Though the olive crop fails, and the fields produce no food,*
> *Though there are no sheep in the pen and no cattle in the stalls,*
> *Yet I will rejoice in the Lord, I will be joyful in God my savior.*

The Sovereign Lord is my strength (Habakkuk 3:17-19).

We must read His Word to understand both His will and the promises we can claim. We should worship so we begin to know Him better. We need to pray for wisdom and power to walk worthy of Him. Having done everything we know to do, we can then plant our feet and stand firmly in Him. Martin Luther said it thus: "Here I stand. I can do no otherwise. God help me." One of my favorite mottos says it in a different way: "Here I take my stand. I will not be moved!"

This is spiritual warfare. It is saying yes to Jesus. It means standing firm in Him and on His Word, and refusing to listen to the lies that Satan tries to plant in our minds. It means that, when the worries pile up and everything seems hopeless, and it appears as if we have nowhere left to turn, we run to the Rock and stand square in the middle.

Ask Jesus to remind you that He is in control whenever you begin to worry. When He does, and He will, praise Him for His concern and provision. The next time it happens, even five minutes later, praise Him once more for all He has done and all He will yet do. Do this again—and again—and again—until you find yourself able to rest in His care. As the old hymn says, "It matters to Him about you!"

When referring to spiritual warfare, many people cite Jesus' words to Peter in Matthew 16:18: *On this rock I will build my church, and the gates of hell will not overcome it.* We visualize a church besieged on all sides by evil, but we thank God the doors will hold because of our Lord's promise. This is not the picture He presented at all.

Gates are not offensive weapons, but defensive. Gates never attack anyone. They just stay where they are put and try to keep from being knocked down! The victorious picture Jesus meant for us to have is of Satan's kingdom besieged and surrounded. The inhabitants are trembling and overwhelmed; their confidence is shaken. The gates will not hold. God has already said so. From below, a trumpet call is heard and God's forces storm the city. The kingdom of God claims victory, Satan's forces are defeated, and Jesus is firmly in control. This is spiritual warfare. This is the powerful position you inherited when you became a child of God. Stand Firm. It is your right.

CHAPTER ELEVEN

Accepting His Faithfulness

*Trials are not enemies of faith
but are opportunities to prove
God's faithfulness.*

~ Author unknown

I put my trust in the Lord while yet a teenager, and He has always been faithful to me. Nevertheless, for much of my life, I believed if I could only trust—just a little more—I would become worthy enough to receive His help. I refused to come to Him in weakness, but tried to appear strong so He would bless me. I'd forgotten that His strength is perfected in our weakness (see 2 Corinthians 12:9).

Seeking medical help, taking medication, or simply admitting to another person that I had a problem would have been "to accept defeat" and prove myself faithless. It would mean acknowledging to myself that I was not a "good enough" Christian to depend on God to make me well. I needed to learn that His grace was never a result of my behavior. There was absolutely nothing I could do to make Him love me any more than He already did.

Perhaps that is why God allowed my illness. He didn't want His child to travel through life, not understanding how precious she was. So He allowed me to be weak, that I might seek His strength. Because I was dependent, I came to God on His terms. I learned to know Him for who He was, instead of who I'd thought Him to be. I found He was not at all the ruthless judge and slave driver I had imagined, but a loving Father, personally interested in me.

We often try to pen God in with our own expectations of who He is. Jesus Himself commented on it in Matthew 11:16,17:

> *To what can I compare this generation? They are like children sitting in the market places, and calling out to others: "We played the flute for you, and you did not dance; we sang a dirge, and you did not mourn."*

Jesus always refuses to dance to our tunes. He rejects every effort on our part to put Him in a box, and consequently, He doesn't always operate the way we expect Him to. Allowing me to think that He had set me free because I had drummed up enough faith to be "good enough" ran contrary to His nature. There is no way you or I can work hard enough to gain more grace from God.

He wanted me to simply believe and trust. I could have rested in His peace and strengthened myself with His joy. Instead, I fell into the trap of measuring faith by performance, rather than His Word. He longed for me to understand that I could never be good enough or try hard enough to earn favors from Him. My performance had nothing to do with His grace. Any special blessings granted me were simply because of His great love.

My worthiness is not what made His grace and mercy a reality. He chose to bless me because He was **God**, not because I was **good**.

We must understand that we live by grace through our faith in an omnipotent and very personal God. We are not, and can never be, set free by our own performance. As I stated earlier, when Jesus said, "It is finished!" that is exactly what He meant. Deliverance has already been accomplished at the cross. It requires no help from us.

ॐ

God taught me a wonderful lesson on grace through my first car accident. I was sixteen and seated proudly behind the wheel of my father's brand new Cadillac convertible. I had just received my license and was ready to drive my mom to the store for the first time. The car had a spotless white top, and a finish of metallic turquoise with flecks of silver that sparkled in the sun. It was beautiful. With Mom in the passenger seat, I drove to the end of the block. I stopped and looked carefully before making a right-hand turn. At the height of the turn, the driver's door flew open. While I reached with my left hand to close it, my right hand held the steering wheel pulled all the way over, continuing the turn.

The car ran over a sidewalk and through a chain link fence. You could hear metal screeching against metal as the fence lifted and tore deep scratches across the hood like giant fingernails. Fabric ripped as the fence continued over the convertible top, then metal squealed again as it came down over the trunk. Paralyzed, I stared straight ahead as the car moved forward. We were inches from our neighbor's dining room window when my mother, using her most authoritarian voice, commanded, "Nancy LoRayne—You stop this car!"

After the police filled out their reports, we returned home. Mom sent me in alone to talk to my father. As I approached our front door, I felt as though I were on death row and taking that final walk. He would be waiting on the other side and I was guilty without excuse. The accident didn't even involve another car. It was wholly my fault. What could I say?

I opened the door, and as I went into the house, I began to cry. Dad looked up from the newspaper and asked what was wrong. With tears and sobs, I blurted out that I'd had a wreck. I will never forget what happened next. Dad was on his feet in an instant, I was in his arms, and he wanted to know if I was all right. He never even asked about the car and didn't seem to care. It was enough that I was safe.

It's like that with God's grace. He really doesn't care what we've done along the way, as long as we're safe with Him now. He longs to pour out blessings and love on us, but He always remains God. He doesn't jump when we snap our fingers or concoct miracles because we think He should. Our walk with Him must be one of faith. He does not require that we always understand what He is doing, only that we trust Him to carry us through the experience. He always has our best interests at heart. 2 Timothy 2:11-13 says it so well:

> *Here is a trustworthy saying:*
> *If we died with Him, we will also live with Him;*
> *If we endure, we will also reign with Him.*

> *If we disown Him, He will also disown us;*
> **If we are faithless, He will remain faithful**
> **for He cannot disown Himself** (emphasis mine).

When we are completely faithless, He still remains faithful:

- When we insist on trying a little harder and struggling a little more to make ourselves worthy.
- When we choose to listen to the Liar instead of the Truth.
- When we refuse to believe that He is all we need.
- When we decide we'd rather "go back to Egypt" instead of allowing Him to lead us into the "Promised Land."

Even then, He remains completely faithful to us. Jeremiah 3:22 (NASV) says, *Return, O faithless sons, I will heal your faithlessness,* while Psalm 103:14 reads, *For He knows how we are formed, He remembers that we are dust.*

God created us. He knows we are only human and that sometimes we fail. He understands that we are not always as faithful as we want to be. He has promised that we can always return and have our hearts healed. He is *the Author **and** Perfecter of your faith* (Hebrews 12:2). As we trust Him, He will complete all that is lacking.

This book is not written to give permission to indulge ourselves, because we are not under the law but under grace (Romans 6:15). God forbid. Our Lord demands holiness from His children. But a pure heart is obtained by resting in Him, not striving after perfection on your own.

This book is written for those who are so deep into self-condemnation that they no longer see the truth. It is for those who have struggled to measure up and failed so often they no longer have strength to lift their faces heavenward. It's written for those, who, as I did, believe themselves to be so worthless that they no longer have any desire to live.

Jesus longs to set you free from the chains of whispered lies Satan has bound you with. He wants you delivered from the burden of your man-made standards of performance. His heart's desire is for you to take your proper place as His beloved, seated with Him at the right hand of God, *far above all rule and authority, power and dominion, and every title that can be given* (Ephesians 1:21, 2:6). He longs to draw you up and out of the pit; to set your feet on a solid rock; to speak peace to your soul.

Jesus offers an invitation too good to be ignored:

> *Come to Me, all you who are weary and burdened, and I will give you rest.*
>
> *Take My yoke upon you, and learn from Me, for I am gentle and humble in heart, and you will find rest for your souls.*
>
> *For My yoke is easy, and My burden is light* (Matthew 11:28-30).

He wants to be your Healer, Counselor, Champion, and Friend. Read His Word. Trust Him. Accept His faithfulness. He longs to set you free. You are His Pearl of Great Price.

EPILOGUE

The Princess

*For He delivered us from the
domain of darkness, and transferred
us to the kingdom of His beloved Son,
in whom we have redemption,
the forgiveness of sins.*

~ *Colossians 1:13,14*

L ong ago, today, and tomorrow, there lived a
princess. She had no idea she was a princess,
because she had been stolen when she was born and
raised as a slave in the Kingdom of Darkness. Her father
loved her deeply and longed for her return to His Kingdom of Light. He thought about her daily, and grieved
over her situation. One day, when the time was ripe, He
called for the Firstborn, Emmanuel, and sent Him to the
Dark Kingdom to redeem her.

In the meantime, Mara, for that was the princess'
name, had grown up. Her life was bitter, she was clothed
in rags, and subject to her evil master's every whim. She
despised her life, her own wickedness, and the master
who controlled her. Sometimes, being the princess she

really was, she would try to throw off her yoke of slavery. She would bathe and dress herself in beautiful garments and set off to do good deeds. But soon she would notice that the garments she had put on were as dirty and ragged as those she had only just discarded, and her good deeds were only selfishness. Her master would laugh. It amused him to watch her trying to break away when she had been completely in his power the whole time.

Everyone imprisoned in the Kingdom of Darkness wore a heavy yoke of chains about their neck. These chains were so bulky and heavy that they greatly interfered with anything the slaves tried to accomplish. No one could feel joyful or at peace, even when resting, because they were so uncomfortable. They made escape from the Kingdom of Darkness absolutely impossible.

The slaves had tried many ways to free themselves from their chains, but it could not be done. Some of the slaves could not remember ever having been free. Indeed, most never had, because they had been born into the Kingdom of Darkness. The yoke had been slung about their necks when they were yet babies. Nevertheless, many slaves cherished their dreams of freedom. Somewhere deep inside they remembered they were really children of the King, and they ached to experience their heritage.

When Emmanuel arrived in the Kingdom of Darkness, it was immediately obvious that He did not wear the yoke of chains. He could move freely where He would and was not subject to the will of Apollyon, the evil prince of Darkness. Emmanuel's clothes were not torn and dirty, but radiated light, and His face was full of joy and peace.

Mara immediately felt drawn to Him. She was intrigued by the fact that He wore no chains, and wondered if He might hold the secret to her own release. He sought her out and taught her many things. "Our Father is the true King," He said. "He sent me from the Kingdom of Light because of His great love for you. He plans for Me to set you free, together with all others who believe." He explained that the yoke of chains she wore would be broken. "You will no longer be subject to the authority of evil Apollyon, but free to accomplish the good works the Father has prepared."

As He spoke, Mara listened intently. She had never met anyone like Emmanuel. She believed He could defeat Apollyon in battle and lead them all forth, unfettered and triumphant.

He had even sealed His words with a special promise: "Your name will no longer be Mara, *Bitterness*, but you will take the name your Father meant you to wear from the beginning. You are a true princess, a child of the King, and Sarah, *Princess*, will be your name."

While many of the slaves loved Emmanuel and believed His teachings, others hated and envied Him because He did not submit to the yoke of slavery, but moved about freely. He stood straight and tall and was not crushed by the heavy burdens the others bore. He spoke to them of freedom, saying that His yoke was easy and His burden light. This only made some of the slaves angrier. They grumbled that, while He promised freedom and rest, they still wore their heavy chains and served their evil master.

One day, a group of the most envious slaves waylaid Emmanuel. They beat Him and dragged Him before Apollyon.

"So you are through hiding amidst my slaves, and have come to me," Apollyon said. "This kingdom was surrendered to me at the dawn of time, and you have no right here. I am master of this place."

"You are master of this kingdom that you acquired through treachery only because My Father has allowed it," Emmanuel replied. "The brief time He permitted you is gone. I am the true Prince of Peace, and it is My right to rule here. You are a usurper!"

"Rule?" Apollyon laughed. "Over a bunch of slaves? They aren't worth your time. Go home, or I will destroy you!"

"The slaves are worth My Father's love and My Blood. I have come to take captivity captive and to set them free. And as for you, though you may bruise My heel, I will crush your head."

With that, Apollyon rushed at Him with fire in his eyes. They tore Emmanuel's robe from His chest, forced Him to His knees; and as He knelt, naked, beaten, and humbled before them all, Apollyon, laughing, drew a knife and plunged it into Emmanuel's heart.

Mara ran forward with a cry and cradled His dying body in her arms. As His blood fell upon her chains, they shattered and fell away from her, though her grief was so great that she didn't notice. She had expected Him to lead the slaves in a battle for freedom. They would have fought and won, and marched victoriously into the Kingdom of Light. Now He lay dying, and all hope was crushed.

While Mara thought about this and looked at Him through her tears, He smiled. With His dying breath He proclaimed: "It is finished. Remember, you are no longer Mara. Your name is Sarah. You are free." As He lay back again, His Spirit left His body.

They took His body from her arms and threw it into a field. Later, when she mastered her grief and went out to wash and bury His body, she couldn't find it, though she searched everywhere. She could only assume that animals had carried it away.

Mara walked back to her room, and her life in the Kingdom of Darkness continued very much as it had before. Her chains had been a part of her for so long that she continued to assume she was bound. She didn't realize they were broken. Apollyon knew it, and knew also that his power was gone forever. He couldn't enslave her again. His only control lay in preventing his slaves from knowing the truth. For this reason, he bound Mara's eyes so she could not see that the chains were gone.

One day, a traveling prophet arrived in the Kingdom of Darkness. He, too, wore no chains about his neck, and Mara chanced to meet him one evening while going about her duties. "I perceive that you have also been freed by Emmanuel," he said as he approached her, for he could see that she had no yoke of chains.

"Alas!" Mara cried, "He would have set me free, but Apollyon murdered Him before my eyes, and now I have no hope but to live out the rest of my life as a slave."

The prophet, seeing what the situation was, reached out gently and unbound her eyes. He placed her hands upon her neck so she could feel there was no chain. "Emanuel has set you free," he proclaimed, "His blood can break the strongest chain, so none of you need to submit to the yoke of slavery. You need only to believe."

Now she knew she was Sarah. She could not contain her joy, and wept with delight. To be truly free, when she had thought herself a slave, was almost beyond compre-hension! She spent many hours with the prophet, who taught her many things.

"Everything that happened was part of the King's plan," he said. "Emmanuel conquered Death itself, came back to life while He lay in the field, and is now ruling with His Father from the Kingdom of Light."

She listened with joy that only increased as she learned more.

"Emmanuel will one day come in power and take His children home so they will be with Him in the flesh as well as in their spirits. But He also wants His loved ones to live victoriously now, so He has promised to live in the hearts of all who love Him. No one needs to be subject to Apol-lyon's evil plans ever again. The King will grant His children power to live righteously and in Truth. Apollyon will never again be able to steal your hope, because a White Dove will come to teach you and bring messages from the King."

Sarah returned home in joy. Her countenance was no longer marred by grief and bitterness, but filled with peace. It was finished! Emmanuel had won!

At times, Apollyon accused her, pointing out her imperfections and telling her that the King could not pos-sibly want someone as lowly and ugly as herself. He was angry and wanted to destroy her.

At these times, Sarah fell on her knees and spoke with Emmanuel. He always heard, the instant any of the King's children called on Him. He would remind her that Apollyon was the Father of Lies, a thief who had stolen her away from her true Father in the begin-ning. He assured her that all she needed to do was rest in His promises and trust Him. He would make her exactly what He knew she could be. He loved her with undying love.

Sarah never again let Apollyon bind her eyes, nor did she submit again to his yoke of slavery. She was not afraid of him, for she knew that she was free and he had no power over her except that which her Father, the King, allowed! The small suffering she endured at his hands served only to make her stronger and more beautiful.

Sarah lived out her days in joy and peace and hope, watching for her Savior's return. She never doubted, though the waiting seemed wearisome at times. She had learned the priceless truth that Jesus, for that is Emmanuel's true name, never fails.

Appendices

One ship drives east and another west,
With the self-same winds that blow
'Tis the set of the sails and not the gales
That determines where they go.
Like the winds of the sea are the ways of fate,
As we voyage along through life;
'Tis the set of a soul that decides its goal
And not the calm or the strife.

~ Ella Wheeler Wilcox ~

APPENDIX I

Becoming a Child of God

K nowing Jesus Christ personally is the most intimate, exciting adventure ever! You will be on speaking terms with the Creator of the universe. He wants to love and protect you, even as He welcomes you into His family and bestows upon you all the rights and privileges of one of His children. Listed below are four points to help you in making this important decision.

1) Man is sinful, separated from God, and unable to establish fellowship with Him by his own works. The Bible says: *For all have sinned and fall short of the glory of God* (Romans 3:23). And also: *All of us have become like one who is unclean, and all our righteous acts are like filthy rags* (Isaiah 64:6a).

2) God loves you personally and wants to have fellowship with you. Consider the following Scriptures:

> *This is love: not that we loved God, but that He loved us and sent His Son as an atoning sacrifice for our sins* (1 John 4:10).

> *But God demonstrates His own love for us, in this: While we were still sinners, Christ died for us...For if, when we were God's enemies, we were reconciled to Him through the death of His Son, how much more...shall we be saved through his life* (Romans 5:8,10)!

3) Jesus Christ has come to set us free from the Law of Sin and Death and to restore us to fellowship with the Father. Contemplate John 14:6:

> *Jesus answered, "I am the way and the truth and the life. No one comes to the Father except through Me."*

While on earth, Jesus told of a sinful, rich man who died and went to Hades. Being in torment, he cried out for someone to dip the tip of a finger in water and cool his tongue. Abraham answered him and said,

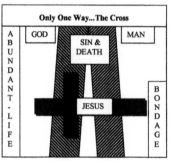

> *between us and you a great chasm has been fixed, so that those who want to go from here to you cannot, nor can anyone cross over from there to us* (Luke 16:26).

Jesus is the *only* way to bridge the chasm of Sin and Death and experience abundant life as God's child.

4) You must personally receive Jesus as your Savior and Lord.

> *Yet to all who received Him, to those who believed in His name, He gave the right to become children of God* (John 1:12)!

> *For God so loved the world, that He gave His one and only Son, that whoever believes in Him shall not perish but have eternal life. For God did not send His Son into the world to condemn the world, but to save the world through Him. Whoever believes in Him is not condemned, but whoever does not believe stands condemned already because he has not believed in the name of God's one and only Son* (John 3:16-18).

Receiving Jesus is done by faith alone. You cannot make yourself good enough to be worthy of His death on the cross. To accept Him, you must simply let go of the reins of your own life and trust Him to accomplish His work of salvation in you. A sample prayer might go something like this:

> *Lord Jesus, I need You! I open the doors to my heart and ask You to come into my life. I am sorry for the wrong things I have done and the many times I have failed You. Thank You that You died to take away my sin and restore me to fellowship with You. I want to become a child of God. Please help me to be faithful.*

If you have sincerely prayed this prayer, Jesus has come into your heart and you are one of God's children. The angels in heaven are rejoicing over your salvation. It is important that you begin to pray and read the Bible, regularly. You will also want to be baptized as an outward act of your obedience and commitment. You will need to find a church where you can fellowship with and learn from other Christians. Don't assume every place that calls itself a church will teach you the truth about Jesus. If their teaching does not line up with God's Word, go somewhere else. There are many fine churches and lovely Christian people out there, and Jesus will help you find one, as you trust Him.

APPENDIX II

What is Bipolar Disorder?

B ipolar disorder*—commonly called manic-depression—is characterized by alternating periods of depression and mania. Persons having this disorder can swing from being overwhelmed with despair and desolation, to feelings of euphoria or anxiety.

Some of the symptoms of the disorder are: sleep disturbances, self-imposed isolation, irritability, loss of interest in hobbies or pet projects, excessive negativity, sexual dysfunction, attacks of rage, and loss of inhibitions. Approximately one percent of the population is afflicted with a severe form of this disorder, while an estimated two percent suffer a milder form of the disease.

---

*Prescription for Nutritional Healing, James and Phyllis Balch, Avery Publishing Group, 1997.

Depression and mania vary in both severity and cycle length. A cycle is the time it takes to go from depression to mania and back again. This can occur within a few hours, days, or in some cases, years.

During a period of depression, the victim is overcome with feelings of hopelessness. He finds it difficult to get out of bed, and may even become suicidal. Some carry on with their regular activities, but inside are full of numbing misery and unable to experience pleasure. Others remain in bed and isolate themselves, not even going to work.

Mania often begins unexpectedly. A person may have boundless energy, restlessness, and a high level of activity. Mental activity is also accelerated, so he may experience delusions, paranoia, feelings of being invincible, and hallucinations. Some may become unreasonably hostile, irritable, and agitated.

The cause of the disorder is not completely understood. Episodes are often triggered by stress. There is evidence to suggest that manic-depressive disorder is biological, caused by a chemical imbalance in the brain. Many believe it is inherited. Wade Berrettini, M.D., Ph.D., is a professor of psychiatry and pharmacology at Thomas Jefferson University in Philadelphia. He states that he and his colleagues,

> *have focused on looking across the entire genome for susceptibility genes for bipolar disorder, and we seem to have found one such gene on chromosome 18. There is already pretty good evidence that there is a gene for susceptibility on chromosome 21.* *

---

*From the Internet, address: *http://www.psych.org/pnews/96-11-01/bipolar.html*

Turkish World Outreach

T urkish World Outreach was founded in 1969, when Steve Hagerman, the U.S. Director, had to leave Turkey because of his bold evangelism among Turks. His passion to tell them about Jesus led to a postal evangelism ministry and a sixty-seven-nation prayer campaign for Turks.

The purpose of TWO is to evangelize Turks by any means possible. Initially, the best means was to invite Turks to know more about Jesus through Gospel Letters sent by Christians. Each month, thousands of Gospel Letters are mailed to Turks throughout the world, telling them about the love of Jesus.

Over the years, TWO has expanded its ministry into the following areas:

- Enabling missionaries to minister in the Turkic world, both with TWO and other agencies
- Planting Turkish churches
- Mobilizing worldwide prayer on behalf of Turks through the "Call to Prayer" and other means
- Sending Gospel Letters that offer Turks a New Testament, *Jesus* video, and prayer
- Assigning Christian Pen-Friends to Turks wanting to improve their English
- Serving Christian workers and agencies working with Turks through free gifts of Scripture, literature, and videos
- Financial support for evangelistic activities of Turkic believers, translation ministries, and Gospel broadcasts

If you would like more information on sending Gospel Letters, becoming a Pen-Friend, praying for Turks, or going to the Turkish World to help establish churches, please contact:

Turkish World Outreach
508 Fruitvale Court
Grand Junction, CO 81504, USA
Phone: (970) 434-1942
Fax: (970) 434-1461
E-mail: *TWO@onlinecol.com*

Order Form

To schedule speaking engagements contact the address below, or to order additional copies of *In The Pit,* use the following order form:

Name: _____

Address: _____

City: _____ State/Prov: _____

Zip/Postal Code: _____ Telephone: _____

_____copies @ 12.95 US/$18.95 Cdn.: $_____

Shipping: ($2.05 first book – $1.00 each add. book) $_____

Total amount enclosed: $_____

Payable by Check or Money Order

Send to: Nancy Hagerman
2976 N. Ronlin Ave.
Grand Junction, CO 81504-4823
hagerman@acsol.net